For Roland
Managed it
once!
Best wishes -
Pete
12th April 2005

Peter Dale

in conversation with

Cynthia Haven

Peter Dale

in conversation with

Cynthia Haven

BETWEEN THE LINES **BTL** BETWEEN THE LINES

First published in 2005 by

BETWEEN THE LINES **BTL** BETWEEN THE LINES

9 Woodstock Road
London N4 3ET
UK

T : +44 (0)20 8374 5526 F : +44 (0)20 8374 5736 E-mail : btluk@aol.com
Website: http://www.interviews-with-poets.com

The Conversation, copyright © 2005 by Peter Dale and Cynthia Haven

'And There Was Light', 'Lead', 'Oriel' and 'Soliloquy', copyright © 2005 by Peter Dale

Artwork on back cover, copyright © 2005 by Philip Hoy

Editorial Matter, copyright © 2005 by Between The Lines

The right of Peter Dale and Cynthia Haven to be identified as joint authors
of this work has been asserted by them in accordance with the
Copyright, Designs and Patents Act of 1988

All rights reserved

A CIP catalogue record for this book is available from the British Library

ISBN 1-903291-13-5

Design and typography: Philip Hoy

Printed and bound by RPM Print & Design
Chichester, West Sussex, PO19 8PR

BETWEEN THE LINES **BTL** BETWEEN THE LINES

EDITORIAL BOARD
Peter Dale Philip Hoy J.D. McClatchy

EDITORIAL ASSISTANT
Ryan Roberts

BTL publishes unusually wide-ranging and unusually deep-going interviews with some of today's most accomplished poets.

Some would deny that any useful purpose is served by putting to a writer questions which are not answered by his or her books. For them, what Yeats called 'the bundle of accident and incoherence that sits down to breakfast' is best left alone, not asked to interrupt its cornflakes, or to set aside its morning paper, while someone with a tape recorder inquires about its life, habits and attitudes.

If we do not share this view, it is not because we endorse Sainte-Beuve's dictum, *tel arbre, tel fruit* — as the tree, so the fruit — but because we understand what Geoffrey Braithwaite was getting at when the author of *Flaubert's Parrot* had him say:

> But if you love a writer, if you depend upon the drip-feed of his intelligence, if you want to pursue him and find him – despite edicts to the contrary – then it's impossible to know too much.

The first twelve volumes, featuring W.D. Snodgrass, Michael Hamburger, Anthony Thwaite, Anthony Hecht, Donald Hall, Thom Gunn, Richard Wilbur, Seamus Heaney, Donald Justice, Ian Hamilton, Charles Simic and John Ashbery respectively, are already available; the next, featuring Mark Strand, is now being prepared. (Further details about the series are given overleaf.)

As well as the interview, each volume contains a sketch of the poet's life and career, a comprehensive bibliography, archival information, and a representative selection of quotations from the poet's critics and reviewers. More recent volumes also contain uncollected poems and a selection of photographs. It is hoped that the results will be of interest to the lay reader and specialist alike.

— Other volumes from BTL —

W.D. Snodgrass
in conversation with
Philip Hoy

Michael Hamburger
in conversation with
Peter Dale

Anthony Thwaite
in conversation with
Peter Dale and Ian Hamilton

Anthony Hecht
in conversation with
Philip Hoy

Donald Hall
in conversation with
Ian Hamilton

Thom Gunn
in conversation with
James Campbell

Richard Wilbur
in conversation with
Peter Dale

Seamus Heaney
in conversation with
Karl Miller

Donald Justice
in conversation with
Philip Hoy

Ian Hamilton
in conversation with
Dan Jacobson

Charles Simic
in conversation with
Michael Hulse

John Ashbery
in conversation with
Mark Ford

Contents

List of Illustrations 9

Acknowledgements 11

A Note on Peter Dale 13

A Note on Cynthia Haven 17

The Conversation 19

Four Poems by Peter Dale

   And There Was Light 91

   Lead 92

   Oriel 93

   Soliloquy 94

Illustrations 95

Bibliography 107

The Critics 129

List of Illustrations

1998, courtesy of Erminia Passannanti © .... Front Cover

Portrait of Peter Dale, II, courtesy of Mike Coleman © .. 12

With Robert Gray, 1956 95

Abinger, 1957 95

Isle of Wight, 1957 96

Prefects' Room, Strode's School, 1958 96

Pauline Strouvelle, 1958 97

Sheringham, late 1950s 97

With Pauline, on their honeymoon, 1963 98

Pauline, with Piers (left) and Kim, 1968 98

1968 99

The Storms, 1968 99

Mortal Fire, 1970 99

François Villon: Selected Poems, 1978 100

Bournemouth, 1982 100

List of Illustrations

Agenda, 26:2, Summer 1988 101

Earth Light, 1991 101

Portrait of Peter Dale, by Eddie Wolfram, 1992 102

In Eddie Wolfram's Studio, London Fields, 1996 102

Edge to Edge, 1996 103

Dante, *The Divine Comedy*, 1996 103

1998, courtesy of Erminia Passannanti © 103

1998, courtesy of Erminia Passannanti © 104

Poems of Jules Laforgue, 2001 105

Under the Breath, 2002 105

ACKNOWLEDGEMENTS

The editors would like to thank the following people: Erminia Passannanti (for permission to use her photographs of Peter Dale); Mike Coleman (for permission to use his portrait of the poet; Anvil Press Poetry Ltd (for permission to reprint 'Platonic' and excerpts from *Edge to Edge)*; Humphrey Clucas (for permission to quote his poem, 'Head Case', which first appeared in *Agenda); and Agenda* itself (for permission to reprint 'Orpheus in Darkness').

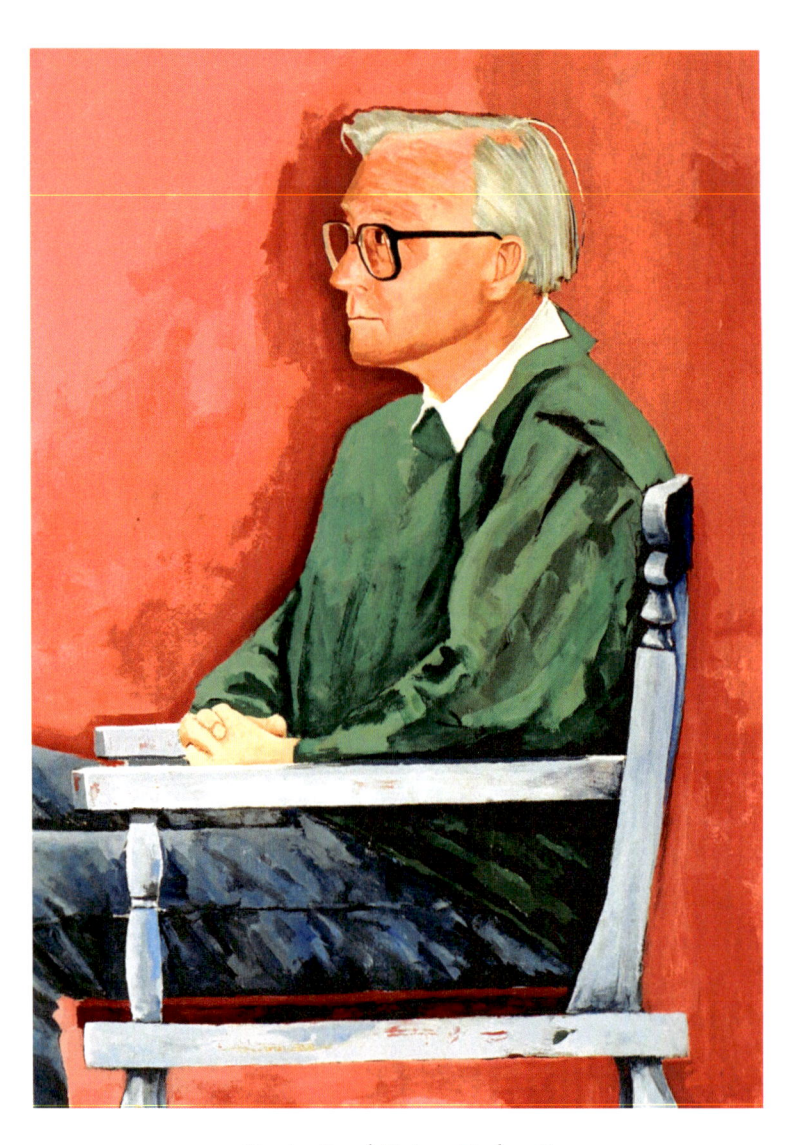

Portrait of Peter Dale, II

acrylic on paper, 59 x 84 cms, 1998
courtesy of the artist
Mike Coleman
©

A Note on Peter Dale

Peter Dale was born in Addlestone, Surrey, on 21st August 1938, the second son of Lena Dale (née Weaver) and first of her second husband Ernest John Dale. From 1950 to 1958, Dale attended the local grammar school, Strode's School for Boys, in nearby Egham. During his first year there his mother died unexpectedly. In 1958, he was awarded a university place delayed until 1960, and in the interim he did his deferred national service in food distribution and ancillary work in hospitals – first locally, then in Oxford. In 1960 he went up to St Peter's College, Oxford, where he read English. He did the usual literary things, helping to run the University Poetry Society, participating in the student magazine scene, and in the course of these activities he met and became friends with Ian Hamilton (who founded *The Review* there in 1962), William Cookson (who had brought his own magazine *Agenda* with him to New College), and Kevin Crossley-Holland (who was to become his first publishing editor). In 1962, the well-known Fantasy Press, based in Oxford, published Dale's student pamphlet of poems, *Walk from the House*. The title poem was a response to the death of his father earlier in the year. This pamphlet received some encouraging reviews; one in the *TLS*, then anonymously written, remarked: 'There is more than embryonic talent here; it is genuine poetry in the making.'

Immediately after graduating, in June 1963, Dale married Pauline Strouvelle. Their son, Piers, was born in September 1964, and their daughter, Kim, in December 1965. Dale taught in secondary education from 1963 until 1993. From 1972, he became joint editor of *Agenda* while also running the English department at Hinchley Wood School in Esher. In this hectic period, as well as writing poems, editing and reviewing, he also produced the bulk of his major translations: the Villon, Laforgue, Corbière and Dante, mentioned below.

While still at college Dale had played a part in persuading William Cookson to shift *Agenda* from its Poundian preoccupations towards a more general approach to contemporary poetry. An extended review section was developed in which Dale became a frequent, and occasionally abrasive voice. *Agenda* became a full-blooded poetry quarterly, later highly respected, particularly for its special issues.

Dale's first full collection of verse, *The Storms*, appeared from Macmillan in 1968. The *TLS*'s reviewer remarked: 'Mr Dale's tough-tender mood becomes trying as poem after poem is spoken warily out of the corner of the mouth.' Writing for the *Times*, Bill Byrom took a somewhat different view: '[These poems] will get themselves read willy nilly, in the end.'

In 1970, Dale received an Arts Council Bursary, and Macmillan published his second book of verse, *Mortal Fire*. As with many second books it was rather amorphous, the work of someone casting about. In 1976 he revised and expanded the book as a selected poems, while retaining its title for American publication. Agenda Editions published it subsequently in the UK. Donald Davie gave this version a very sympathetic review in *The Listener*. Its forward significance was in the new self-contained sequence of love-poems, *The Going*. Here Dale mixed formal verse with free verse, the latter something he had refined when preparing with Kokilam Subbiah versions of the Cankam (or Sangam) poems of classical Tamil. Some of these eventually appeared in *The Seasons of Cankam*, published by Agenda Editions in 1975. *The Going* sounded his earlier intensely lyrical note, moving away from the strand of narrative that was initiated perhaps by his father's death.

This approach next showed itself in the varied yet formal work of a sonnet-sequence, *One Another* (1978), probably his most well known and accessible original work – recently reissued by The Waywiser Press. Of these sonnets, David Storey remarked: 'The best ... are engaging, immediate and direct – to the point where the writer disappears and the reader is confronted intimately with the subject – as though thought and feeling, and observation, derive exclusively within the reader's mind, perception and reaction seamlessly one.'

A somewhat surprising departure in *Mortal Fire* (1976) was a move into verse drama with the play *Cell*. Despite a lack of enthusiasm on the part of reviewers, Dale continued his experiments with *Sephe* (which appeared in *Agenda*, 18.4-19.1) and *The Dark Voyage* (which appeared in *Agenda*, 29.1-2).

In 1982 Agenda Editions published *Too Much of Water*, his only book to date not to contain a sequence. Of the final poem, 'Summer Shadows', Glyn Pursglove wrote: 'it is a major poem in which particularity of observation is perfectly married to a searchingness of mind, in language which, for all its clarity, is richly teasing in its implications.'

Nearly a decade later, *Earth Light* (1991) appeared from Hippopotamus Press. The lyrical intensity is just as evident but two sequences take somewhat new directions. *Mirrors, Windows*, a group of ten terza rima sonnets, deals with the theme of three generations interweaving and reacting to history, events, religion and each other. The second sequence, *Like a Vow,* also in varieties of terza rima, deals with the apparent persistence of memory and landscape.

Edge to Edge: New and Selected Poems appeared in 1996 from Anvil Press, and contained a handful of new poems. Alan Brownjohn described the book as 'a monument to this poet's unfashionable kind of integrity.'

Dale's most recent book of verse, *Under the Breath,* published in 2002, again by Anvil Press, contains another intriguing sequence, *Da Capo,* which built on the techniques employed in *Mirrors, Windows.* A section of dramatic monologues, *Tirades,* contains short stories, song and ballad, and a poem dealing with the highly-charged encounter of Judas with Christ in Hell. Judy Gahagan wrote of the book: 'The first three poems are breathtaking. The unguarded intensity of feeling is transformed by a precision of voice expressing this feeling that has created three truly great elegies.'

Dale's last book from Macmillan was *Villon,* which appeared in 1973. A translation into equivalent verse forms of the great French poet's *The Testament, The Legacy* and other poems, *Villon* was issued in a plush edition illustrated with woodcuts by Michael Denning. Penguin Classics published a revised bilingual edition in 1978, and this was followed by several later impressions with various revisions. Of the 1978 edition, Lawrence Durrell said: 'One despaired of ever finding someone to "capture" him in English. But it's been done. Here it is. Hats off.' Donald Davie was also much impressed: 'It is high time that a volume so important to modern poetry in English be issued in permanent hard covers, in spacious format, and incorporating ... further reflections and second thoughts by the exceptionally thoughtful and enterprising translator.' Philip Howard wrote: '... translations into strict ballade form by Peter Dale ... Miraculously it works.' The translation has been continuously in print since its first appearance. A fully extended and revised bilingual edition, *François Villon: Poems,* appeared from Anvil Press in 2001, along with a similar update of their 1986 edition of Dale's *Jules Laforgue:*

Poems, the first edition of which had moved D. J. Enright to write: 'It isn't merely that Dale's feet fit neatly into Laforgue's shoes, for he contrives to replace a French skin with an English one ... The collection is hard to overpraise.'

To accompany *Edge to Edge* in 1996, Anvil Press published Dale's terza rima version of *The Divine Comedy*, which is now in its fifth impression. David Wheatley remarked of it: 'This is the best complete rhymed Dante we are likely to have for a very long time.'

Though in his younger days a regular reviewer and critic for *Agenda* and other magazines, Dale has never collected his many prose pieces. His only prose book – apart from the interviews he has done for BTL – is *An Introduction to Rhyme*, which was published by Agenda Editions/Bellew in 1998.

Anvil Press published a bilingual edition of his complete translation of Corbière's *Les Amours Jaunes/Wry-blue Loves and Other Poems* early in 2005. This received a Poetry Book Society Recommendation for translation. Of earlier extracts, published in 1985, Stephen Romer remarked: 'Dale's version of "Le Poète Contumace" is very impressive. He rhymes as neatly as the original and in the same places. The tonal quality of Corbière is retained throughout the whole of this long poem.'

Since resigning from *Agenda*, in 1996, Dale has edited a poetry column for *Oxford Today*, the university's magazine for its graduates, supporters, and well-wishers. He was also an initiator with Philip Hoy and Ian Hamilton of BTL.

A Note on Cynthia Haven

Cynthia L. Haven was born in Detroit and educated at the University of Michigan, Ann Arbor, where she studied with the late Joseph Brodsky and earned two prestigious Avery Hopwood Awards for Literature. After receiving her university degree, she moved to London and worked at *Vogue*, *Index on Censorship*, and a short-lived Third World newsweekly on Fleet Street, the *World Times*.

Currently, she is a literary critic at the *San Francisco Chronicle* and writes regularly for the *Times Literary Supplement*, the *Washington Post Book World*, the *Los Angeles Times Book Review*, and the *Cortland Review*. Her work has also been published in *Civilization*, *Commonweal*, and the *Georgia Review*. She has been affiliated with Stanford University for many years, and is a regular contributor to its magazine.

She has received over a dozen literary and journalism awards, and has authored several non-fiction books. Her most recent books are *Joseph Brodsky: Conversations* (University Press of Mississippi, 2003; Adelphi Edizioni, 2005) and the forthcoming *Czeslaw Milosz: Conversations* (University Press of Mississippi).

THE CONVERSATION

What follows is an edited version of written exchanges between Peter Dale and Cynthia Haven which started in October 2003 and ended in December 2004.

The pace of your readings and speaking engagements has increased in the last few months. This is always rewarding for a poet – but do you have any insight into what is causing this renewed interest?

As a freelance now, I'm more available. While I was teaching full-time many requests had to be turned down because timing or venue was impossible. If you do that fairly often news gets around that it's a waste of time inviting you.

On the other hand, working on the magazine *Agenda* in those teaching days hardly helped to make me flavour of the month.

In the last century, we watched some of our most celebrated poets sinking into suicide, alcoholism, nervous breakdowns, and bouts of madness. You've said in the past that poetry is not only, as Eliot termed it, 'a mug's game', but for some, a game of Russian roulette. But your life, like Richard Wilbur's, has been eminently sane – 30 years of full-time teaching (many of them running a big department), as well as writing, editing an important poetry review, translating, raising a family, and so on. How have you managed that?

The answer seems to be that I've always tried to follow a saying of Dr Johnson's to the effect that if you are idle you should not be solitary and if you are solitary you should not be idle. I became a workaholic to fend off the occupational hazard of manic depression. The second answer is that I married Pauline, a down-to-earth, eminently sane woman. Nevertheless, I think the incidence of madness among poets and of the other evils you mention may be somewhat exaggerated. One in eight hospital beds here is psychiatric, I read somewhere recently. It's probably about the same percentage of disturbance among poets.

Perhaps I take a bit of a dismissive view of this because Alvarez in the Sixties and Seventies was pushing his theories about extremism in literature – which seemed about as far and fallacious as romanticism could go. Ian Hamilton's introduction to the *Oxford Companion to Twentieth Century Poetry* has more statistics about the assumed prevalence of aber-

19

rant behaviour among poets, but they don't really show it as a necessary or majority professional qualification, though his figures, of course, only refer to mentions of such problems with poets included in the book.

Perhaps post-war influences were more unbalancing than usual, but history has always been an ongoing catalogue of horrors. Valéry's psyche was odd enough but he remarks that everyone in the world has been happy and unhappy and that extremes of joy like those of sorrow have not been withheld from the grossest and least singing of souls. Life may be hell for more than just writers and artists and the freedom to act within those hells may be more circumscribed to most ordinary people. At the same time, one remembers Plato on madness and poets. And there may be 'normal' ways of being mad. An American psychologist in the Seventies remarked that anyone who appeared normal in America must be mad. You could say the same here.

In the U.S., most poets, particularly important ones, have university appointments. This system has other obvious weaknesses – Dana Gioia pointed out some in his much-attacked essay, 'Can Poetry Matter?' Instead, you've been a schoolteacher, which would certainly be an anomalous situation in the U.S., though I understand it is less so in the U.K.

A good few writers do school-teaching here, if only in their beginnings or as stop-gaps, though quite a number are full-time, as I was. Auden springs to mind, though he liked it for largely non-teaching reasons – the easy adulation of boys. If you're a creative writer, wherever you teach or work will lead to compromises. The long vacations initially look like untrammelled time purchased for writing. It's never as accommodating as that, but at least it's easier than working year round in an office or factory – or chasing commissions and deadlines.

The lack of hassle over money was the biggest benefit for me. Several of my friends and contemporaries who went freelance had very difficult lives in that respect. It meant I never had to write anything I didn't want to write. Also, I hadn't much time to spend, as you may do when freelance, moping about over whether another poem was ever going to turn up.

University teachers may have more chance of proselytizing for their own work and sending disciples out to preach but that too has drawbacks. I was never much bothered by budding poets wanting an instant stamp of approval for their latest. The odd parent occasionally tried it.

When he was asked if he taught creative writing, Joseph Brodsky used to say, 'No, I teach creative reading.'

That's it. I don't really believe you can teach or be taught creative writing. If would-be writers haven't sufficient *nous* and commitment, if they don't have that inner determination that they are writers and know what they want to achieve, then anything that a creative writing course is likely to give would merely lead them to a species of imitation. Keats said that the genius of poetry must work out its own salvation in a man. He was right. However, a good creative writing group might mend a few holes in your literary education or awareness. After all, even such an apparently simple thing as rhyme is to a large extent learnt, and not just a question of sound. There are culturally acquired components to it and it varies subtly from language to language. The structure of sonnets can be learnt but not how to write 'Leda and the Swan'. Any aspiring writers in a creative reading group may acquire something from that type of information and may also read something new, or something old in a new light, that will make them admire and do otherwise.

In an interview with Ian Hamilton (Agenda, 31.2, 1993) you said, 'Well, with teaching I am kept away from writing most of the time. But things happen under pressure in the mind that one's barely conscious of, I suppose.' That sounds rather indefinite and 'iffy'; do you have any more definite observations about those 'things that happen'?

The whole endeavour to make poems is 'iffy'. The initiation of a poem seems to be largely below the level of consciousness. Sometimes, when working flat out in education and with *Agenda*, I'd feel a sort of mind pressure, a presentiment that a poem was 'out there', about to settle, and in a day or so a word or two of it, a rhythm or image would land. You learnt to make space for the landing. Who can say whether those work pressures more or less released the subconscious mind to get on with poems – prevented the literary intelligence from intervening too early? Or whether there would have been more or different poems if I had been freelance?

In the same interview, you said, 'it's a kind of lunatic concept to have a career poet because you can't base a career on what is virtually a form of "luck".'

Eliot said every poem was an epitaph – hardly a career prospect. It's what you do with that 'luck', the *donné*, that counts. No job fully protects you from the fecklessness of it. Sometimes a poem would 'turn up' while I was teaching. It was a rare piece of luck to be able to set the class a piece of work while enough of it could be jotted down. I like to work in absolute silence, which is hardly what a classroom has to offer. (During invigilations the odd epigram could be managed. There are about a hundred or so unpublished ones.) A poet's luck may depend on a sort of vigilance. On the other hand, poems may be like those things forgotten in 'senior moments'. They often come back into the head when you stop fretting about them. As I said, the biggest benefit a job gave was in not having to worry over money too much. That, I think, improved my luck.

Here's another comment you made then: 'Poetry isn't subject to the will and the intention, and one has to wait and one may wait for ever and nothing come.' It's pretty close to the idea of inspiration and the muse, isn't it?'

I was distantly referring to Shelley's 'A Defence of Poetry': 'A man cannot say, "I will compose poetry." The greatest poet even cannot say it; for the mind in creation is as a fading coal which some invisible influence, like an inconstant wind, awakens to transitory brightness ...' Also to Coleridge's famous attempt to define the act of composing in *Biographia Literaria*, chapter 14. Then there was Keats, who said poetry should come as naturally as the leaves to the tree. All three, of course, were romantics, but the classical Valéry's experience seems to run parallel. (Nothing said about poetry is ever a hundred-percent true. Most poets have experienced picking up an old discarded draft for lack of a *donné* and finding it suddenly take flight. Hardy did quite a bit of that.) Once the words start coming, the literary intelligence kicks in, and sometimes it does so too soon. But until something 'arrives' you just have to be patient. You can't will a *donné* into existence. You have to be alert for it to surface anywhere, anyhow and any time. Trying to force it seldom works. Once arrived, as Coleridge says, it comes under the will and understanding and is retained under their irremissive, though gentle and unnoticed, control.

Aren't poetry's origins, after all, close to incantation?

Words frequently come into the head like an incantation from some disembodied voice – sometimes, in my case, a female voice. Valéry claims that 'The Pythoness/La Pythie' grew out of a single given line.

Brodsky, again, may have some insight here:

*The shape of a girl, for each man, is surely
His soul's shape – you, Muse, can confirm this richly –
Implying love's source but, alas, love's ruin,
For souls have no bodies...*

This may sound overly whimsical – but can you think of any other reason the incantation should come with a female voice?

Brodsky is often over the top – but I've no idea why it should sometimes sound like a woman's voice. Perhaps voices as well as images may sometimes be eidetic. It's certainly one I don't know and I rather resent her intrusion: you feel the poems are somehow not quite your own. Akhmatova spoke to her visible night visitant:

> I say:
> 'Was it you that dictated to Dante the pages
> Of Hell?' And she replies: 'I am the one.'

Perhaps I should try talking back like that.

So, you begin with sound...

Yes, poems are made of words, words are partly made of sounds and when they come together they create rhythm. It seems to me that it is usually the rhythm of a phrase or line that will carry the conviction. I sometimes wonder if people, with all the visual media now surrounding them, can hear the words as they read them silently (as was previously the usual case from the way we were taught first to read aloud and then to internalize). If you can't get the rhythm right for the poem nothing else will work. I hate it in public readings if I speak a word wrongly. It feels like a waste of time to continue with that poem, like a broken string in a violin concerto. The spell is broken.

Browning speaks of composers making out of three sounds not a fourth sound, but a star. It's much the same in poetry.

Yes, it is. I quote that passage from 'Abt Vogler' in an unpublished verse-essay on Villon. It's the most succinct way of putting the sort of poetic magic that occurs in a real poem. I first read that poem in the sixth form, so the idea has been with me a long time.

Another comment from Ian Hamilton: 'I think I believed that by writing that poem, there might be some mitigation of [another's] suffering. One knew that in life ordinary speech made little difference, couldn't save the other person from death or from illness. Poetic speech might work differently. Some magic seemed to be required. While writing a poem, one could have the illusion that one was talking in a magic way to the subject of the poem. One might even think that this is doing some good, making things better. And then, of course, you know it isn't. You wake up and find it hasn't.' That comes awfully close to Auden's remark about poetry making nothing happen.

But Ian's illusion for poetry – while he was writing the poem – is of something much more powerful in its effect than Auden's various views allowed for. Auden speaks, for example, of poetry's function in disabusing people of falsenesses; of its role in clearly expressing a state of being in two minds. Ian is close to Auden only in recognizing the ineffectiveness of poems once they exist. While Ian thought the poem might mitigate someone's suffering he was *compelled* to write it as powerfully as he could. But you could easily be less committed to disabusing people of errors or be in two minds about expressing a state of being in two minds. I tend to agree with what Frost said when a similar question was put to him about the effect of poetry. He asked what sort of hurry the questioner was in for anything to happen. It may be a very slow process.
 I prefer something else Auden said, which is that the arts are our only means of communication with the dead and that without that communication a fully human life is not possible. That's poetry doing something. But the mystery remains: you read a well-made poem and little happens in your mind's eye and ear. You read another, flawed as it may seem, and yet it moves you powerfully. There's an inexplicable x factor. A real poem suspends for a time the internal exile in the skull, awakens a dead poet's voice. It's that x factor we're all after.

You were born in 1938, so your early years were the years of World War II.

Our house was about three miles from Vickers aircraft factory, where my father worked during the Second World War; the main London to Portsmouth railway line passed close by it. The small town was twenty miles from central London. All were targets for German bombers. Not too comfortable a location. There was an anti-aircraft gun just behind the infants' school I attended and a factory making airscrews. I remember a barrage balloon landing in the field opposite the house.

What sort of family was it you were born into?

It was a poorish, working-class, evangelical household. The elder of two boys of a second marriage, I've an eldest half-sister; my elder half-brother died in 2003. My younger brother died a few years earlier. The religious input came from my father, and handfuls of salt came from my mother. Both of my brothers were sporty, team-game crazy. Left-handed, I was called 'cack-handed' at their games. I was introvert, bookish, reticent – but I was also a good cyclist, so I used to get away.

Can you say something about your father's religion? It figures in a lot of your early poems.

My father was a strict Fundamentalist, a Salvationist, and his religion tended to isolate us from the rest of our neighbourhood. My sporty brothers shook off his influence and religion faster than I did because they left school early. I did three years in the sixth-form – which means I left in 1958, almost twenty years of age, still more or less financially dependent on him and therefore much closer to his influence, though school had soon distanced me from most of his ideas. This fraught relationship was intensified by the fact that my mother died when I was just gone twelve; he was lonely and thus emotionally much more possessive. Her handfuls of salt were in danger of losing their savour. He died when I was away at college, which is another reason why my home background is difficult to define now, because I never had that mature relationship with parents which usually fills people in about their childhood and upbringing.

What a lonely childhood! At the time, it must have seemed to you totally normal, totally average, as one's own childhood usually does...

Yes, as a child you think your home-life the sort of home-life that everyone has. As an adult you look back and wonder what truly was going on. This is particularly so of a second-marriage family life. My father encouraged us, after his fashion, in educational matters, and all three boys actually won entrance to Strode's School. Until my mother died I thought that I was happy enough and that the other children were. Looking back,

I'm not so sure about that or my parents. I know now that my mother tried at least once to commit suicide. I can see now how her husband might have been a contributing factor. But it was all a long time ago.

You were born in Surrey, and went to school in Surrey. Was Strode's a day school or boarding school?

It was a pretty intensive day-school with a small intake of sixty boys divided from the second year on into science and Latin streams. I went on the Latin side despite a fascination for physics – in which I would have been hampered by my low mathematical ceiling.

Egham, where the school was, borders Runnymede, where the Magna Carta was signed. I understand there are old Bronze Age settlements there. So it's rather a historic place. Did its history affect you at all?

As sixth-formers we were allowed to wander in school lunch hours on Runnymede and, above it, Cooper's Hill, made famous by the royalist poet Denham in the seventeenth century. In the poem 'Cooper's Hill' he prophesied that eternal monuments should stand on the hill – and incidentally started a fashion for 'Hill' poems. It now has the impressive Royal Air Force War Memorial, and further down is the Magna Carta Memorial, 'Freedom under Law' – quite a good description of metrics. The school itself had been founded in 1702 to educate poor children of the district by a philanthropic member of the Worshipful Company of Coopers which was still represented on the governing body. A Founder's Day Church Service was held annually in the parish church, which I believe is a Wren church, certainly one influenced that way. So, yes, we were surrounded with history. Poetically too: Denham had lived nearby on St Anne's Hill, which I cycled over to school. Matthew Arnold had lived nearby in Cobham and Laleham, where he was buried, just along the river Thames. So I was surrounded by history, and it all imbued a sense of continuities, cycles and repetitions, or, as Wordsworth phrased it, 'the goings-on of life'.

Before going to Oxford you spent a couple of years in hospitals, working as a porter and as an orderly in operating rooms. I take it that brush with mortality, even if from an onlooker's point of view, must have been bracing preparation for your life as a poet?

I'm not sure whether the foundations weren't already laid by then. My mother's death was an early brush with mortality; she used to mention 'Sonny', her boy who had died in the previous marriage: just a name, no snapshots, even. A neighbour-friend's baby died of diphtheria when I was about six. And of course the war dominated my first six years. Every bang and crump was a bomb landing nearer in a child's imagination. We kids confused germs and Germans in our minds. The milkman's electric float could sound like the start of the air-raid siren. There were producer-gas trolleys behind the buses that occasionally went bang and scared the daylights out of us.

Billy Collins said in a talk he gave at Stanford in November 2003 that if you took all the poems about death out of the Norton Anthology, you'd be left with the Norton Pamphlet.

When I was teaching an exam anthology, one of the fifth-formers said: 'Why do poets always write about autumn?' I answered: 'Look again: when they don't, they write about death.'

A number of your earlier poems focus on hospital scenes – 'Elegy,' 'Meditation Down the Wards,' 'Patient in a Ward'. Often, you focus on the helplessness of visitors:

> *Awkward and hushed,*
> *they try a smile,*
> *then shift and fidget, stood without dignity*
> *at the beck and call of junior nurse or maid,*
> *shielding their flowers, helpless, almost afraid.*

Hospital work, which I did instead of National Service, was a shock after being brought up cushioned in a grammar school and indoctrinated at home with the idea of a good and compassionate god. Yeats, whom I studied in the sixth-form, had disapproved of passive suffering in poetry: I became interested in trying to see if it could be decently done somehow.

Was Yeats a major influence for you?

In those early days, yes, he must have been. Four poets we studied intensively in the sixth-form were Keats, Hopkins, Hardy and Yeats. These were in addition to Shakespeare and Chaucer, of course. Yeats's rhythms, formal skills and his use of chorus lines interested me then, but the mumbo-jumbo and a certain braggadocio in parts of his work are more than I can take now.

What does it mean to suffer passively in poetry – and what does suffering 'decently' mean to you?

'Decently' is a tricky word. I supposed that Yeats meant, in the light of his lines about when a man is fighting mad, that active courage, wounded heroism, not the fortitude or the heroism of the overpowered – whether by force or other circumstances – was the true topic for poetry. He had identified a problem. A poem about someone else's suffering can seem voyeuristic or sadistic, or it can appear to be presenting the poet as a sensitive soul. It can seem to intrude on privacy and to be side-lining the victim. The Christian idea that helping the sick without compassion is some sort of failing also won't wash. A starving person does not care in what mood the food is given so long as he gets some. Brecht and General Booth, founder of the Salvation Army, both said versions of: *bread first, then ethics*. So writing of suffering is difficult, and I was probably too young to do it decently, but it seemed that one would have to concentrate on the inadequacy of any response one can give – an inadequacy that pastors consoling the bereaved must often feel. The inadequacy of words seems to be greatest when faced with such things.

You were a student at Oxford University from 1960 to 1963, though you worked in the city of Oxford from 1959. That was a lively time, and a period of much social and political change.

Yes, the threat of nuclear war, the Campaign for Nuclear Disarmament, the Cuban Missile Crisis and so forth – and, as ever, the student's usual chronic shortage of cash that often limited activity or involvement. But there was the sexual revolution, too, and a great creative and critical ferment in literature. Oxford at that time seemed to be bursting with the idea of the small literary magazine. Ian Hamilton had started one at school. At Oxford, he founded *Tomorrow* and then *The Review*. Michael Horovitz started *New Departures* there. Student magazines appeared, such as *Gemini, Oxford Opinion, Isis* and *Cherwell*. And of course there was *Agenda*, founded by William Cookson while *he* was still a schoolboy. Then there was Jon Silkin, who used to arrive from Leeds to sell his magazine *Stand* around the colleges, and slept on Ian's sofa while he stayed with us – my bed-sit and Ian's being next door to each other. The Fantasy Press revived for a while, bringing out a series of six poetry pamphlets.

Much seemed to be happening. Would-be poets of every persuasion swanned about the place. William, Ian and I, to mention only three, were very short of cash, living on educational awards – barely enough to live on, much less support literary magazines.

And you were trying to get a degree as well. Can you say something about your undergraduate studies?

The literature syllabus by the time I arrived had inched from about 1830 up to 1900. I used to joke about its historical approach, misappropriating and adjusting Yeats: 'Whatever's written in what poet's name.' Graduate students could cheat a bit by regarding as permissible game those born up to that date. You still needed Latin and maths to matriculate and had to do Anglo-Saxon and Middle English for an English honours degree. I was hardly conscious of literary issues in academic teaching – the sorts of theory which have since had such far-reaching and probably insidious effects. Looking back, it seems we arrived more or less as indoctrinated sub-Leavisite, New-Critical types, while scarcely knowing it. It took considerable efforts to move away from all that. Ian referred to his college days once as 'pre-literate'. I know what he meant. I sometimes think mine were spent sleepwalking.

Few dons seemed very aware of, or sympathetic to, American poetry – or modern British, come to that. John Bayley was very supportive of William and *Agenda*, though I didn't meet him at that time.

My own 'reverend' tutor did tedious lectures on Virgil's influence in English Literature. Not that I went to many lectures by anyone. They're a pretty inefficient way to learn most things. The student magazine *Isis* got into trouble with the university for trying to review lectures.

You couldn't gauge Oxford by the tutors I had then. I'd unwittingly first encountered the reverend as a bowdlerizing editor of our school texts, the Warwick or Hereford Shakespeares, if I remember the series right. He was past it, even objected to my typing my essays. Larkin had had tutes with him at St Peter's during the war: 'a tutor I disliked from the start,' he said in a letter. Absolutely right. Ian Hamilton told me later that the reverend was briefly the American poet Michael Fried's supervisor as well – so that would be three poets he antagonized. Some of my grammar-school teachers seemed intellectual giants by comparison.

So when did you 'decide' to become a poet? Was it a decision?

From fairly early on, when I was in my mid-teens, I knew I was going to be a poet. It became a conscious intention long before I knew what the ramifications of such a decision might be. The urge to create began as something long before it focused on writing. My father wanted me to learn to play the organ. We had a small harmonium in the house. As I said, I'm left-handed, but the right hand is inextricably linked somehow, so that it's always trying to mimic the left hand's movements. This makes keyboards tricky. Besides I hated the tutor and was not very musical.

Yet it triggered something and, even though I was a musical incompetent, I tried to write my own tunes. They weren't any good, of course, but there was this strange hankering to do something of the sort. I tried oil painting and was marginally less incompetent. Then the English master read us 'To Daffodils' by Herrick – a strange choice for a boys' school. He remarked on the difficulty of speaking directly in such a tricky form. That evening, I wrote about six verses, to Herrick's two, rhymed in the same form but not about daffodils. The master was a bit miffed when I showed them to him, but I was hooked. I parodied the school song, and several of the hymns sung in assembly, and then I began writing things for myself. I was fourteen at the time.

Did anyone else in the family show any interest in poetry?

After her death, I discovered that my mother had kept some of her babybook on my brother's development in verse. My elder brother wrote light verse to celebrate occasions in his own family, and tended, I think, to look on my published stuff as inferior.

Your 'unbookish father' bought you your first book of poetry – Spender's Collected, I believe. When was that?

For my fifteenth or sixteenth birthday. I was by then subscribing to the London Magazine and both the public and the school libraries kept me well supplied with books.

Talking of Spender, you once said, 'He was probably a better influence, bad as he was, than Dylan Thomas. He led to Auden.' I occasionally notice an echo of Auden in your poems, such as 'Coastwise': 'Yet I would tell you if I could.' Has Auden been a major influence for you?

Later on he became a sort of subterranean, largely technical influence. I like many of his Thirties poems, though fewer of the later ones. He was a master technician and craftsman whose skills I studied, the poet most referred to in my book on rhyme. His later garrulousness was wearing, and his psychological obsessions and religious leanings did not interest me.

Hopkins said that the effect on him of a masterpiece was to make him admire and do otherwise. Otherwise is a good influence.

You began with Herrick imitations ...

Only one. That was enough.

So what was your first 'real' poem?

The first attempt that made me feel I was getting anywhere was 'Meditation Down the Wards', which I'm still sufficiently fond of to keep in print.

That's pretty impressive for a first poem. Already a harbinger of things to come – in its preoccupation, for example, with the ordinariness of suffering and grief, and its reference to 'the pseudo-smile I try in fear and guilt.' Even the questioning, stoic agnosticism of 'I'm a coward if I daren't / insist their pain's a pointless accident.'

Religion tried to make some sort of moral sense of the suffering of living things. It didn't make any moral sense to me, however, so I suppose that poem closes the chapter on my father's influence. The daring comes in feeling that the poem presents a pretty bleak view of life for one so young.

What was your first published poem?

My first properly published poem was a couple of quatrains called 'Duologue', which appeared in an art magazine, *Painter and Sculptor*, in 1958. That was curiously precursory, too, dealing with two views of the same event in dialogue shape.

That seems an odd place for a first appearance of a poem.

Immediately after school, waiting to go to college, I printed a booklet that contained both these poems, among others. It was appallingly badly set, in monotype, on an ancient hand-press with a chase only just wide enough for a ten-point pentameter. In hindsight, the booklet was rightly called *Nerve*, but only because those were the only uppercase letters I

31

had that were large enough for titling. Oddly, and for some reason now forgotten, I named the author 'Peter J. Dale', in the American style – a style I also kept for a few months at college, where some namesakes lurked. *Nerve* was printed somewhat hastily because I was to share a London art exhibition with a painter, a draughtsman, a sculptor, and a musician friend. The poems, handwritten in Indian ink on hardboard, were framed and hung between the paintings. There were strong links with the visual arts in my beginnings as a writer, hence the appeal of imagism. Anyway, to come back to your question: it was as a result of the painter Eddie Wolfram's interest that the poem was published in *Painter and Sculptor*.

So far, we don't have too clear a picture of where Dale-the-young-poet comes from. Apart from the things you've already mentioned, what reading, learning, whatever, shaped you as a poet?

I did the scholarship papers and hence an extra year in the sixth-form, and we were encouraged to read widely. (I did Pope in the entrance paper; a fairly untypical poet in education then.) I was a voracious reader of all and anything, the Angry Young Men, the Existentialists, masses of science books, philosophy. The Latin/library master had this secret, brilliant wheeze to further our general education by flattery. He appointed library prefects and set them to read inspection copies to check their suitability for library inclusion. He'd also take you wandering round the shelves and tell you what science, linguistics, and philosophy to read.

The origins of the poetry bug are always obscure. My early pre-college enthusiasms were Hopkins, Browning, Arnold, Auden, Pound, Owen, Yeats. I won a Collected Dylan Thomas in the sixth form, but soon tired of him. The English master timetabled me once a week to read Milton aloud, alone in the canteen. That was great training in rhythms. 'Make the cutlery rattle.' He tried to get me to read Shelley but I found his choice of poems too ethereal. I wanted a more down-to-earth approach – 'I met murder on the way. / It had a face like Castlereagh' – that side of Shelley. I used a Peacock quote in my defence – it went something like: 'very few men of genius have said or done in their youth with so terrible a gravity as many foolish things as Shelley.'

When and how did you meet Pauline Strouvelle? Since many of your poems are love poems – and that rarest of birds, poems celebrating long love – it seems appropriate that we discuss her a bit.

I met Pauline at some Plymouth Brethren do for teenagers. We were about fifteen. There weren't many secular places for the sexes to meet then. Most schools were still single-sex.

Plymouth Brethren? Then her religious upbringing was perhaps a little unconventional, too?

No. She had a completely secular, sensible upbringing and was probably doing the teenage thing visiting such a place to irritate her parents. It didn't last. The Plymouth Brethren I always supposed were the puritans who could not get a booking on the founding boats to America. In fact they were founded by a Dubliner, I'm told, in Plymouth in the 1830s. They split into several internecine sects here in the usual way. Their first split was as early as the late 1840s. But they would not have rocked the boat to America too much.

And did she really have a saffron skirt? 'Oh, my love, / frivol of hesitation in the slow peal / of the skirt.' That was in 'One Off' in One Another of 1978; *and this miraculous skirt re-appears nearly a quarter of a century later, in your 2002 collection, with a whole poem of its own, 'The Skirt'!*

It was nothing to do with her – there are lots of skirts in the world. Anyway, we fetch from the mini-skirt era. I like bright colours, except for myself. I once had my classroom painted bright orange, and the girls called it the morning-sickness room.

In your interview with Richard Wilbur, you described his wife Charlotte as the 'perfect wife of a poet.'

Not quite. He told me that Willa Muir had called her 'a perfect poet's wife'. I suggested moving the adjective to the correct place. But I could not have survived as a teacher or poet without Pauline's perfectly unobtrusive support.

She's not a writer. Is she a great reader?

She's a great reader of prose, of all sorts. Not verse, though. She prefers Shakespeare on stage. Music is her first love.

Maybe that isn't such a bad thing. Not to be entirely lost in words – as your dedication to her in Mortal Fire *says: 'yet find no words, / none like your presence.' She certainly appears to be a muse.*

I suppose she must be some sort of a muse, if such things exist. But as for that ethereal metaphor, the idea of it would amuse – and bemuse – her. She's too down-to-earth for that. She does proofread when necessary and makes the odd penetrating criticism of draft poems, the more acute sometimes because she's not in the trade. After my old friend Roland John had read *Da Capo*, he dropped me a line to say he didn't think I'd be writing any more poetry because in that sequence I had killed off my muse. Fortunately, at least for me, he was wrong.

You've mentioned that she's a gardener – presumably that's the reason for all the roses, wild flowers and crocuses in your poems? I also note the prominence of sparrows, martins, hawks, thrushes, and other birds in your work. In 'Bats,' for example, the heroine is 'obsessed with birds'...

England's full of gardener women and gardener men. The American writer Wallace Kaufman, a friend of mine at Oxford who was doing Wordsworth research, remarked to me back then that when he arrived here he suddenly understood the English poets much better because he discovered they all live in a 'garden'.
    Much of the natural imagery derives from my cycling days all over the Downs, the Thames Valley, the Cotswolds, the Mendips, the Chilterns, and the Isle of Wight, and from walking tours I used to do with Kenneth Crowhurst, to the memory of whom *Under the Breath* is dedicated. But the gardening imagery may go back to my childhood. My mother had varicose ulcers and was therefore not very active. The family seldom all worked at anything together. But once, when I had mumps, aged about seven, they all worked together in our neglected back-garden while I was stuck inside, still small enough to stand on the window sill and watch the lively goings-on. That afternoon has stuck in my imagination. That event may also go some way to account for the number of windows in the works.

And the birds?

The penchant for observing birds probably derives from the fact that an aunt gave me an illustrated book of birds when I was about seven and I became expert at drawing them from constant copying, a skill long since lost.

I seem to remember squirrels in a number of your poems – even a brooch in the shape of a squirrel, in one.

I used to like squirrels; my children gave me fluffy ornamental ones annually on my birthdays: nice cheap easy things for them to buy. As a kid, I used to watch endangered red squirrels on my paper-round. The grey varmints got in my roof recently and it cost me £1,500 to get them out and keep them out. That squint-eyed one that sneaked into the poem sits on my monitor. That's probably my true muse. I call him Yossarian.

Why Yossarian? He makes a curious muse...

Well, Yossarian couldn't live without strong misgivings. That squirrel squints at me and keeps the poems away from delirium tremens. Didn't the real Yossarian struggle to dream the right dreams for the psychologist? Perhaps that's what poets are up to, in a way.

In one poem you watch as thrushes 'divebomb the basking cat'. Cats seem to figure prominently in your poems as well. In the 1988 issue of Agenda *which was devoted to you, I also note there are two poems dedicated to you which are about cats. Are you a cat lover, perhaps?*

I have always thought that there are cat-poets and dog-poets. I'm one of the former. To misquote *Macbeth*, even Shakespeare didn't like poor cats being kept in adages. Our own cat used to make quite clear when it was time for me to stop writing because she wanted her night's sleep in my/her chair. Prose is dogged; poetry is feline.

Some have called you a poet of the countryside – which you are – but your oeuvre seems to focus even more on human relationships – 'to see oneself as another', as you wrote in your essay on Burnshaw. This certainly seems to be a theme in, say, your sonnet sequence, One Another, *and in* Mirrors, Windows, *also.*

Your quotation's on target: the epigraph of my first collection was Blake's 'The most sublime act is to set another before you' – humanity going against evolutionary propensities. Sequences and plays offered more space to explore these things from various angles. Perhaps my work is a long footnote to either version of Auden's: 'We must love one another or die/ and die.'
   What interests me is how humans interact, and how difficult it is to

35

communicate clearly things like past events, mood, feeling and memory, the mix of feelings and ideas they live in. I've usually concentrated on manageable twosomes. The natural world impinges on these interactions because we often make relations, celebrate and experience things in natural settings which then gather resonances that we *variously* carry with us. A good teacher is someone who can teach a class of thirty in such a way that each pupil feels you are teaching him or her alone. That makes a big set of twosomes.

So then, empathy is at the heart of your work – perhaps even a motivation for it?

Empathy's vital to all the arts and life itself; first in the artist and then in the perceiver of the work. I admire Milton technically as a poet but only have an intermittent empathy with the personality emanating from his work. There are lesser poets I have more empathy with. There are also characters in works of art, not necessarily satire, that produce in the reader levels and stages of antipathy, even revulsion.

Can you give a few examples on both sides?

Some of the characters in Browning's dramatic monologues are pretty repulsive, but he keeps your interest in them alive. The Keats fragment, 'This moving hand …' hits me emotionally more than most of Milton. It's a concentrated drama.

May I ask what you make of this, from W.S. Milne: 'Language, for Dale, is a remnant of that order in which facts of domesticity and the events of friendship, love and death are still marginally reconciled.'

I'm not sure what that means. What order is he speaking of? Why should language be a remnant of anything? I don't write 'language' per se; what I am trying to do is present experience in ways that are 'truable' in a reader's mind. How could single poets reconcile such vast abstractions and to what? It makes me want to reach for my A. J. Ayer.

It's always dangerous to associate the poet with the narrative voice in his poems, and yet there must be much of your father in your sequence, 'Mirrors, Windows', in which 'a middle-aged man observes his dead father's features in his reflection in the window pane'. Your reference to the father in the poem as 'old Bible ham' suggests as much.

I put a note in *Edge to Edge* about this, which says 'Hindsight suggests that the difficulties of the father-son relationship are more general than personal.' The issue was not my father but religion. That's why a lot of detail was cut out of the reprint of 'Unaddressed Letter' and 'The Fragments'.

I don't follow. Why, because it was too personal?

I find those poems hard to talk about. It's partly the period of time they stir up and partly the mess of three attempts at exorcism. Rewriting after years is probably always a mistake. I should have learnt this from Auden's example or Lowell's, and ditched the poems completely. The mindset was mine, but most of what seems to others biographical detail is not actual but imaginative construct. It *might* conceivably have happened, if my father had lived on, but he did not and it never did.

By the time of *Edge to Edge*, I wanted the poem to be more universal. My view was that even the dead are entitled to their privacy, and certainly should not have it transmogrified in such a way. So that note of mine also says I returned to the *theme* in the poem you mention. In *Mirrors, Windows*, everything is imagined, thus allowing me to play around with the three voices of three generations which weave in and out of each section in ever-changing relationships, as they do in life. I was surrounded as a kid by bible hams. The whole sequence is an imaginative construct to approach that generational theme.

I'd always been fascinated with Yeats's remark about an age being the reversal of an age; I suppose that, for the last few hundred years at least, offspring have revolted against their upbringing in various ways. The New Apocalypse is followed by Empsonian intellection; the Movement is followed by Extremism and that by the Ludic and so on.

On the question of the biographical input in the arts: imagine someone's actual life as a stained-glass window. What happens to it in a work of art is that the panes get broken up and shaken in a kaleidoscope with other slivers of lives observed and imagined until it makes other patterns. Any attempt at separating the elements and putting them back where they started is a tricky process, probably impossible, even for the artist, given the nature of the subconscious and instinctive elements in the arts. In the end, ideally but seldom in reality, the poem should survive freestanding, as an entity on the page and in the ear. It must, in some way, universalize experience in the mind of the reader.

Eliot has that famous passage on this mosaic activity of the imagination:

Why ... do certain images recur, charged with emotion, rather than others? The song of one bird, the leap of one fish, at a particular place and time, the scent of one flower, an old woman on a German mountain path, six ruffians seen through an open window playing cards at night at a small French railway junction where there was a water-mill.

Bits of this, changed, show up among much else in 'The Journey of the Magi', but they don't make it a 'biographical' poem. It's still a dramatic monologue.

A poet needs to imagine, feel and write things *as if* they are personal; that way they have a chance of being real to others. People nowadays seem to give more credence to a poem if it feels personal to them. That does not prevent a lyric poet presenting character dramatically like a playwright; it does not preclude the multiplying of personality. To misquote myself imperatively, the injunction is: 'Poet, you make the darkness personal.' This is not a position taken up by cogitation; it is what developed as the poems did.

Let's try to piece together a few of the shards, then, and see if we come up with anything interesting. You write:

You never heard me speak, not a single instance.

And:

*I promise nothing; we shall miscomprehend
each other and possibly do much worse.*

Do I detect a certain amount of the usual father-son misunderstanding here – or was it more than usual?

It's the usual thing. Those quotations are dramatic, not biographical, part of the attempt to depict lyrically and dramatically how the generations inter-react. My father did read my first poems and helped me set up a home press. He may even have been an unwitting influence in pushing me into words in the first place with his habit of remarking, of a hymn or Bible text that he liked, 'Those are beautiful words.' This used to puzzle me, and at a fairly early age I wondered to myself whether it was the words or the thoughts that were beautiful. The idea of words being beautiful was a mystery. It made me wonder how words in themselves could be or might be 'beautiful' – or 'ugly', come to that. It made me aware of words as examinable, considerable 'things'.

The issues in the poem hover round religion because I had sufficient background to feel confident with the material. As I said, I'd been surrounded by Bible hams as a kid, some more sympathetic than others.

I notice the repeated image of hands – 'A handyman, is it, now?'– 'Your hand, man, from the grave...' – 'Give me your hand; you never gave me a hand'. There's an unexpected St. Veronica reference as well: 'fashioned without hands'.

Some Catholic ideas and imagery were used to develop dissensions in the poem, as with the argument about intercession with and by the dead. I'm no Catholic or Protestant. The poem needed those ideas. It's the sort of thing Protestants and Catholics argue about. I could have used transubstantiation and consubstantiation, I suppose.

Someone – I can't recall who – suggested that it's your own father who enjoins you to 'get yourself an obsession', referring to religion. Is that another case of mistaken identity?

It's not my father's injunction; it's a character in a poem who says that. Nor is it specific to religion. It may even hark back to the Samuel Johnson nostrum I referred to earlier on. At one level, the passage it occurs in should be read as a sort of parallel to Polonius's advice to Laertes, which Shakespeare is sending up. The final couplet of that sonnet reveals with a touch of irony the speaker's uncertainty about his value as adviser or example: 'no date for your diary'. – That hints at other levels, too.

If I'm not getting too intrusive, you do seem to dance around the issue undecidedly. More recently, in 'Briefing':

> *(Some say that even God*
> *was forced to be a man*
> *to crack what flesh and blood*
> *and good and evil mean.)*

That's a great image of yours. One of the jobs of the arts is to dance around issues. Keats presented the idea that poets remained in uncertainty about most things. I tend to agree, but not on this issue, where I'm an incorrigible materialist. Yossarian, who could not live without strong misgivings, is my muse, as I said earlier.

In the passage you cite, for example, I *qua* I am not the speaker: it's a ghost in waiting, given to irony, in a ballad monologue, a dramatic invention. I think I first came across the idea you quote in my teens in Chesterton. The same dramatic point would be true of 'A Woman Speaks to God the Father':

> 'I am jealous of you, God.
> If I had every inch your might,
> in my black hole you'd spoil your rod;
> you'd kick up stars in endless night.'

That poem in a woman's voice came complete during the night, except for one word, which I changed days later. 'To kick up daisies' is a British idiom meaning to be dead. Way back, the daisy, or day's eye, was that star, the sun. Stephen Hawking once said that maybe the purpose of the universe was the creation of black holes; counting then, there was one per 36,000 cubic light-years of space, an astronomical crowd.

That poem, you say, 'came complete during the night', with the exception of one word. You mean you actually composed this poem in a dream, and it wasn't simply the idea that occurred in a dream?

I woke, nipped into the study and wrote it down in one go. Once you wake you can't vouch for a dream. All I know is that the dream woke me with those words in my head and that my conscious mind hadn't put them there. In that draft, 'endless' was a metrically weak 'perpetual', presumably a memory of 'nox perpetua'.

What's interesting in the two sequences mentioned earlier is that the 'other' you are trying to understand is no fictional invention, no abstract emotional construct – or at least doesn't appear to be. Am I mistaken in thinking that, in One Another, the woman bears more than a passing resemblance to your own wife?

Yes, you are. That answer will make other people want to ask, as my father-in-law once did: Who, then, is this woman? The character, as suggested by the stained-glass image I used above, is an amalgam of experience, imagination and observation. There's also an input from the visual arts, particularly oil paintings.

A fictional character has to be imagined clearly and in enough detail to feel real and authentic to a reader. If that result's achieved here, as you seem to imply, that's what I was after.

The character in One Another *dies – obviously, not your very-much-alive wife.*

Recent retrospection has left me wondering whether the close of the sequence, the grieving, may have derived from a transposed delayed reaction to my mother's death when I'd just gone twelve.
   As I said earlier, you have to write *as if* it is personal, as if it is 'truable' in the reader's perception of the poem. The imagination can do this. Shakespeare did not have to live through everything he eventually dramatized. Writing it was a form of living it, I suppose, in the end. Look what Dante did with almost only a name: Beatrice.

But how does what you've just been saying square with what you said in an interview you gave in 2001, where you declared 'There is biography in my work. Too much, in some of it ...'

I was, I think, referring to some of those early poems such as 'The Fragments' that we've already touched on, with those elements of apparent biography.

And now the tables have turned: poems about fathers have given way to poems about sons, which have a more optimistic tone. I'm thinking of such poems as 'Starting Your Travels', 'Damages', and 'Coastwise'. A very different mindset from that behind the father poems: 'I shall know how to comfort you in time / and it shall comfort you in time.'

The speaker is not specified; it could easily be a woman, in fact. The situation is universal, presenting how we would like to comfort our infants if we could. But the poem may not be as optimistic as all that. The 'black-moss dark' is contrasted almost as a positive against the 'terror of the light'. We keep children in the dark about many things.

I know Auden and the New Critics maintained that you shouldn't need to know the life to evaluate the work, that biography and art should be kept in separate boxes. Still, so many poets today write from a confessional or autobiographical point of view. I recently reviewed a book of poetry impossible to evaluate without knowing a little about what was happening in the poet's life. It's not all that uncommon. Can you tell us your position on this?

My position would be that if biography is what the poet needs to write about in a particular poem then the lines should contain enough of it to make the poem free-standing, not leave it pointing as a mere signpost to somewhere else. There's no obligation to be biographical; some of the confessional stuff of the Sixties is not so much autobiography as an attempt to outplath Plath. It's not an issue I would go to the wall about. But I have a sneaking suspicion that we might find Dante, Villon, Shakespeare, say, less intriguing, less interesting if we knew more about their biographies. Instinctively I feel the converse is unlikely. The position may be different again with other poets. Perhaps Lowell would seem a better poet if we knew less about him. Larkin's letters seem to have spoilt his poems for some people.

The Keats fragment you mentioned earlier provides a fascinating case in point.

It does. We think we know it is about Keats' illness and Fanny Brawne. It is powerful and totally effective without our knowing that. Indeed, an early editor of his work reckoned that it might be a fragment of a subsequently lost Elizabethan or Jacobean text which attracted him enough to be copied out. The poem feels alive – that is the word. It can stand free of biography. That freedom is what my taste or compulsion is after. 'The poem is not distinguished in its source.' Would the poem be weaker if we did discover it was Elizabethan?

So much poetry has focused on romantic love, passionate love. Do you find that your father-son poems – 'Unaddressed Letter', 'The Fragments', 'Signature' – are relatively unexplored poetic territory?

Not really – and maybe we should include daughters, like Plath. What about Henry IV and Hal? Hamlet and the Ghost, Lear and his daughters? Gloucester and his sons? Edmund Gosse's prose treatment, *Father and Son*, is powerful. Dylan Thomas touched on the theme, particularly in 'Do not go gentle'. Similarly, Lowell dealt with his father as did Ian. We shared the experience of early parental deaths. Hugo Williams, David Harsent and several others on this side of the Atlantic have also dealt with the father-son theme.

But still, those are a few isolated examples, and a few of them are plays.

Perhaps I'm saying that I think you turned over some new ground in Mirrors, Windows.

Perhaps I got more of all sides of the issues into a tight space without tidying it lifelessly up. I used a similar technique later, in Da Capo.

I'll take your point about autobiography, but maybe we could go back again to the poem 'Fragments', which at the very least returns you to your father's religion, if not to your father. It begins with a Salvation Army hymn. You've said it 'deals with the whole idea of the tradition of Christianity in the modern world' Do you mean by the juxtaposition of bible-thumping religion and the images of the Holocaust? The distribution of fundamentalist tracts in a bus queue with the queues in concentration camp? With the juxtaposition with 6,000,000 Jews dead and '6,000,000 Guinness drunk every day'?

Yes. There is that thread in it. That hymn epigraph was meant with a measure of irony; the drinking imagery from an organization so teetotal that it had rejected the communion service. It links to the last remarks on Guinness. The nuclear problem is touched on in the section, 'I chanced to tread ...', originally title poem of *Walk from the House*. The 'stellar dust' ideas in that section, I seem to remember, ultimately derive from a remark cited in *The White Goddess*: '... [A] fundamental tenet of the Church, that Jesus's material body was immaterialized at the Ascension had ... been spectacularly disproved at Hiroshima ... [A]nyone with the least scientific perception must realize that any such break-down of matter would have caused an explosion large enough to wreck the entire Middle East.' It's odd where poets scrounge their ideas, and what they do with them. So, it was a typically youthfully ambitious piece, trying for a range of reference, from Shakespeare's *King John*, to the idealist philosophers, to *The Waste Land*, medicine, and so forth.

I'm curious: two of the poems in your latest collection, Under the Breath, *end with a scream – 'Short Story' and 'Mottled'. Admittedly, it's a 'wordless scream' in the latter; and a comment, 'Only the dead may safely scream', in the former. Would you care to comment on this?*

Everyone lives, said Thoreau, lives of quiet desperation: why aren't they screaming? Larkin asked the same question of 'The Old Fools'. In another poem, I wrote: 'Dear, we must cry more quietly.' In evolutionary terms, a scream must mean easy prey for scavengers and hunters.

'Mottled' is a beautiful poem, with its 'rarish bird, / some grouse-like kind, / rich mottled feathers like a Christmas cake.' How did it come about?

I was travelling up to London and passing the tedium by trying to recall where and when I'd seen this particular bird. When I realized it was in a dream, the first two stanzas came readily into my head, spreading out either way from 'But it had been a dream.' I thought the poem was finished. Then, one morning, more than a year later, when I was word-processing some Dante, the last verse came into my head and I just typed it into Dante and then copied it across files.

Earlier, you said, '... working on the magazine Agenda *in those teaching days hardly helped to make me flavour of the month'. Certainly there are perils to the life of the poet-critic. How many punches have you had to take?*

Or pull? There's no way of knowing the answer to that. You know mostly how you slogged on to so little purpose. There are sometimes highly visible and vocal dust-ups but the literary world is probably more adept at the subtler ways of putting you down and doing the dirty than most other trades. Paranoia is almost endemic. Most of the reactions are invisible: the anthologies you're not in; the readings and reviews you didn't get; the publications you couldn't bring out; the anonymous publishers' readers who put the boot in – all or none of these things may be part of this. Such things also happen straightforwardly. There's no way of seeing any of this clearly when you are in the thick of it. You hear things on the grapevine but those snippets may also be part of other hidden agendas and machinations, or not. In the end you can only say your say wherever you can.

I remember speaking with Randall Jarrell's wife, Mary, and she mentioned that there were many people who wouldn't speak to them because of his criticism. Have you found that to be the case?

Now and then. I've sometimes learnt circuitously that I've peeved the odd poet, editor or critic.

Does it contribute to a sort of reclusiveness?

I suppose so. Maybe you couldn't speak so straight if you didn't start off as a recluse and stay that way a bit. (What was it Horace wrote? "I have to put up with a lot, to please the touchy breed of poets.") But other things contributed. I'm fairly reclusive by nature. William was more at home with correspondents than with people directly. He developed a vast correspondence and thus 'knew' a lot of people and something of what went on. Writers would drop into the office while I couldn't be there since I taught full time. I'd less time and inclination for correspondence than William, confined my letters largely to editorial matters, and so I was reclusive even on paper. I seldom had time to go to literary dos.

The critic Donald Davie called Agenda *the best literary periodical of its kind in Britain. So there were bouquets as well as brickbats.*

We had quite a bit of both. What do any of them mean or ultimately amount to?

You've taken on some of the heavyweights in your criticism.

Yes, and dozens of lightweights.

Lightweights tend to be forgotten on their own. But some of the heavyweights are still very visible – John Berryman and Robert Lowell, for example. You skewered both in some of your reviews.

I wouldn't say I'd skewered them, exactly. An alternate view was vigorously put.

Some of your remarks about Lowell's use in his poems of conversations and letters – particularly those of his wife Elizabeth Hardwick – echo Elizabeth Bishop's well-known criticism: 'Art just isn't worth that much'. You wrote: 'The thought that they [his family, ex-wife, and friends] assent to this treatment worries; the thought that they do not, horrifies.' Like Bishop, you quarrelled with the idea that being a poet 'excuses all kinds of human betrayal, weakness, narcissism, and self-pity ...'

Poets, like bee-keepers, may have an unusual talent, but that doesn't give any of them more rights, fewer responsibilities than any other person. Nor does it give them privileged rights over any other person. If anyone's likely to be stung, it's their job to be stung first. People tend to give artists and celebrities more allowance than they deserve. I'm with Bishop there.

Nonetheless, saying that took courage.

In hindsight it may look like courage or foolhardiness but at the time we just went ahead with the job in hand. We didn't think criticism should be a respecter of persons. Contemporary judgments of contemporaries are so wayward and faddish that we didn't think anyone should be given preferential treatment. Of course, if I'd known personally what troubled people they were I might have given them a miss altogether. It was the policy on *Agenda* to review without fear or favour; quite a few 'names' got drubbings; several were virtually ignored.

British reviewing then tended to be more abrasive than most American was, though Jarrell's an obvious exception. I remember some British reviewer remarking that here a writer is assumed guilty until proved innocent whereas in the States a writer is assumed innocent until proved guilty. I recall one American writing to me, saying that if the Atlantic hadn't been in the way he would have hopped over and bumped me off for the views I'd expressed on Berryman's *Delusions, Etc.*, in the US magazine, *The Saturday Review*. I think Ted Hughes once cancelled his subscription to *Agenda* over something I said. William used to try to keep such reactions from me.

I wrote a poem of apology to Lowell, unfortunately finished just after he died. I thought some degree of apology due when I was caught in the same bind as he was over rewrites. An American poet friend thought it a cave-in and criticized me for that poem, too, so you can't win. The poem still keeps a critical distance, I think.

In that poem you do seem to recant a bit –

> *Considered long, too late expressed,*
> *I breathe this brief apology*
> *and covet with keener jealousy*
> *your incommunicado rest.*

There's a degree of irony in 'incommunicado'. I hope. And I do later remark:

> Rest, rest, immortal spirit, rest
> upon your laurels once again

which remains ambivalent. He did appear to rest too easily on them sometimes, though I don't know how much his mental troubles should take of the responsibility for that. That 'immortal' is also tempered by the last line: 'where straight deletion's much the best'. The previous quotation derives from: 'rest, rest, perturbed spirit' in *Hamlet*. I do like quite a few of Lowell's poems, but not so many of the shapeless sonnets.

Did you really covet his 'incommunicado rest' – or am I making too much of this 'jealousy'?

At the time I was deeply depressed and one view of 'incommunicado rest' is death. The first occurrence of the word 'jealousy' merely refers to the fact that big publishers can give more leeway to their selling authors' second thoughts than other authors may expect from smaller outfits. I don't think anyone could really be jealous of Lowell; no one could wish for his anguished life just to write a poem or two.

How do you juggle the responsibilities of the reviewer with the needs of the poet?

It's almost impossible to do so. Poets review from their own perspective, which is seldom fair to other poets. On top of that, reviewers of whatever bent are seldom these days given enough space to put a case cogently. There may also be literary wars and skirmishes going on and you may be misperceived as taking sides. There's a more subtle problem, too. Readers aware of your prose may be misled by its methods and its tone to expect similarities with and direct reflections of those qualities in the poems with the risk that they may misread what is in the verse, misjudge what's what, and mistake what you are trying to achieve.

Has this happened to you? Could you give an example or two?

My early reviewing was fairly abrasive, acerbic, ironic, forthright. Most of the poetry is much more quietly spoken, more sidling in its effects, so the prose may have been a misleading signpost to the verse for some people. I can't give any very specific examples, but from aspects of various reviews over the years I think I've been at least partially misread in odd ways, and not only by unfavourable reviewers. In addition, some recent reviewers seem not to be up to the mark with many of the formal aspects of verse. It can be the poet's 'fault', I suppose. You might not expect the author of 'The Fragments' later to turn out a poem such as 'Like a Vow', or what have you. Edward Thomas at first signed his poems 'Edward Eastaway' to obviate this very problem.

Grey Gowrie wrote in his preface to the 1997 Agenda *anthology: 'To run a magazine of poetry for 35 years is a perverse and heroic undertaking. You cannot do it without passion and something of the loneliness of disciple or long-distance lover.' Does that comment resonate with you in any way?*

I don't think discipleship comes into it. Grey was doing a bit of special pleading to excuse William's infatuation with Pound. Passion certainly comes into it, particularly at the outset, but that would also include strong aversions, too, at that stage. If you do it well it's bound to be fairly lonely; friends, even when they don't make it overt, tend to assume that you'll favour their work over unknowns and are miffed when you don't. People you reject a couple of times or so tend to resent your cheek. It's better then to keep yourself at a distance. It helps if you are reticent. But life is so fleeting. You don't see what you've been up to or missing till it's too late to reflect or change things much. The real writing life's a lonely one. There's a lot of bonhomie and conviviality around the edges, though, and some writers enjoy that or cope with it better than others. Some writers are virtually destroyed by it, as Dylan Thomas probably was.

You've mentioned William Cookson already several times. His death earlier this year must have been a blow for you.

It was a blow when he died. He was as strong as an ox for most of his life. I never expected to be around when he wasn't.

How did your friendship begin?

That's a long story. We'd both gone up to Oxford the same year. He saw a poem of mine in *Oxford Opinion*, a student magazine, and mentioned his enthusiasm to another poet about town, Michael O'Higgins, who'd met me, I think, through working together at the Radcliffe Infirmary. Hearing William speak of his enthusiasm, Michael introduced us. William reprinted the poem, never collected, in *Agenda* 2.6. From then on, William and I worked on the magazine with bungee-like connection until I left it in 1996.

And so you became absorbed in Agenda.

Gradually. From Oxford, 1962 on, I had a backstage role, one of the influences that persuaded William to add a proper review section of contemporaries and also to move the magazine away from Pound's political and monetary obsessions into poetry proper. I'd refused to work for the magazine if it maintained these lines, wanting it to be a poetry magazine at the cutting edge. William, in our immediate post-college days, spent a lot of time in correspondence with me, trying to get my name on the editorial page. I somewhat bumptiously spent as long resisting the idea, wanting to keep my independence. I can only remember one of my baiting phrases now, about not wanting to be swamped in 'the all-dissolving detergent called MacDiarmid', one of William's literary heroes. I reviewed and published verse in the magazine from college days on, becoming 'official' about 1972.

What sort of person was Cookson?

William was amazing in all sorts of ways. He looked a good deal like a young undissipated Dylan Thomas. He founded *Agenda* while still in the sixth-form, as I said earlier. He had encountered Pound's *Selected Poems* in the fifth form in 1955. A year later he had given Pound's *Thrones* volume of *The Cantos* an insightful review in the school magazine. Consequent correspondence with Pound led to their first meeting in 1958. This encounter – a sort of road-to-Damascus experience that made him a Pound devotee for life – persuaded him to found *Agenda* to forward the whole range of Pound's ideas and link his cognoscenti. Pound gave William initial impetus and purpose, the confidence to have a go, but Pound's influence, though it remained, was only one. William's widowed mother was also a strong influence in this direction. His father had founded the magazine *English*.

Such conviction and commitment was in many respects to be of great benefit to *Agenda*, as it would be to any small magazine, but it became to varying degrees its limitation. Like Pound, William would never bend to received opinion or media attention regarding a poet's quality, but he bowed only too readily to Pound's views. In my early days, I admired quite a bit in Pound's poetics and literary journalism but not much else in his ragbag of ideas. Someone said Pound could not think but had a magpie's attraction for bright ideas – and not so bright, too.

But Pound's influence did have its positive aspects?

Well, as I say, it was in some ways limiting, but without some such obsession in an editor most small magazines only survive for a few issues. Outside the Poundian modernist spectrum, it left William open to suggestion as an editor since so much lay outside his chosen path. In consequence he was happy to invite the participation of various guest editors, though not always happy with the results. In my view, it became deleterious when William began to edge some Poundian political rather than poetic judgments back into the magazine. (I had a heck of a job persuading him to print a Geoffrey Hill essay that criticized Pound.) Aficionados of Pound – of various quality – could get a voice in its pages somewhat easily. One of these aficionados even accused me of being employed by MI5 when I kept a dotty piece by her from appearing. This blinkering also made it difficult for William himself to move the magazine beyond the modernist period into more contemporary fields. William's view of what a serious editor should do in furthering genuine poetry did indeed affect the magazine's pecuniary fortunes, and it eventually lost it its Arts Council funding. William was never going to be dictated to about the contents and appearance of his magazine. Commitment and conviction can sometimes become stubborn intransigence. To give a simple example: among other things, he would never agree to indexing the magazine though he bound it to last. He was obstinately careless of volume and issue numbers on the spine. The result is that a shelf of white *Agendas* is a reference nightmare. He also persisted, against all advice, in doing double issues that crossed volume numbers, so that library binding was problematic.

But for the association to have lasted as long as it did, there must have been some serious areas of agreement?

We both thought the poem on the page and in the mind's ear the first and final thing to be regarded. We were always united on that and on many poets.

You've mentioned Cookson's willingness to make space in the pages of the magazine for Pound's political views, and said how deleterious you thought this. Can you say a bit more about this? Am I right in thinking that it was this issue which led to your resigning from the magazine?

In 1996, without showing me what he was up to, William put out an editorial note defending Mussolini. It was a long footnote, indeed, added to a friend's review of a book of Poundian essays. The reviewer dealt in some detail with one by William himself. This gave William the excuse for his intervention. What annoyed me over and above the content was his labelling it as an 'editorial note'. We were supposedly *co*-editors. This was the last of many straws that eventually broke the camel's back.

William was reverting to the dotty areas where the magazine began, perhaps an effect of his alcoholism. Of this particular issue I had only seen seventeen pages before he went to press. We remained good friends, but I'd had enough of his high-handedness.

And had too much of his alcoholism?

That was certainly a big additional problem. From the mid-Eighties until it became a contributory factor to his early death, William fought a sad, depressing, running battle with the condition. It made working on *Agenda* difficult for all who helped.

It sounds like a very up-and-down friendship.

Other friends remarked that we used to bicker over issues like an ancient married pair. So yes, it was up and down. All relationships between friends with strong convictions and determinations are a bit up and down, though. We were united by a mad passion for poetry. It looks madder now than it felt then. To both of us it was a total commitment. We both had a good sense of humour. That enabled us to make allowances for each other and usually defused situations. Besides, William was fond of my verse, and in those days there was some sort of rapport between us, two loners with a liking for people who stood at odd angles to the universe. But it was this to-and-fro between us that gave the magazine its variety and zip, when it had it. We agreed about many poets and poetic issues, so that was a sort of cement.

A long-lasting cement, apparently. I note that, in 1996, you dedicated your Edge to Edge: New and Selected Poems *to him...*

William was very reluctant to let me resign; even after I had, he tried to find a formula to get my name back on the editorial page. The dedication was a small expression of thanks at the end of our working relationship for his long-term and continuing support. He had kept me going as a poet in my busy teaching years.

Let's explore another friendship. You've said that Ian Hamilton was one of your oldest poet friends. How did that friendship come about?

I met Ian before I met William, in the Oxford University Poetry Society, I think in 1959. He was a year in advance of me; he'd also done National

Service, so we were older than most of the other students. In the Cuban crisis, the student living in the next room to Ian's, a Trotskyite, had rushed off in Spanish-Civil-War fashion to defend Cuba. Ian suggested that I take over his room, which I did. From then on we became close friends, showed each other our drafts and had detailed discussions over them and current literary issues.

In the mid-Seventies – what with his involvement with *The New Review* and the Lowell biography, and mine with a big teaching department and editing *Agenda* – we lost touch for a time, but not for long. We ended up in the Eighties and Nineties living about four miles apart. Shortly after I resigned from *Agenda*, we both worked together with Philip Hoy, setting up Between the Lines. This amazed some of Ian's other friends because they thought he had long since lost his former commitment to and energy for that sort of thing.

I notice that you've written several poems for him – I'm thinking particularly of your recent one, 'Not Another Dedication', that ends so movingly:

> Something ingrained in our war-child years:
> tears were the thing to fight against
> when drained of every other strength.
> And now these words instead of tears.

That elegy was written and added to *Under the Breath* at the last-minute proof stage – always a risky thing to do. In our early days, Ian used to complain of my penchant for rhyming and I would respond with complaints of his ineptness at it. I teased him about this again in the festschrift for him, *Another Round at the Pillars*. Here, again, in the opening verse, using two different sorts to move the 'vicious circle' back to those student days and to the long search for the perfect timeless poem. The 'long perspective' is a glance at a line of Larkin's.

That 'not another' in the title presumably refers to your first dedication, also a poem, in your first book, The Storms, *in 1968.*

Yes. That first dedicatory poem was to mark our friendship and to acknowledge that he had been first publisher of the title poem. (William was very peeved that I'd let Ian have it instead of *Agenda*.) The exact form of that dedication came about in a strange way. He said he couldn't review a book if it were dedicated to him, so we agreed on a compromise. I hid his name acrostically in Anglo-Saxon metrics so that he could review the book – which he did in his usual underwhelmed way. He also complained that I had anticipated for the book the title he wanted for his of 1970. For *Edge to Edge* we decided the acrostic might as well be highlighted. The other poem in *Under the Breath*, 'Away Break', was written when I'd been transcribing the tapes of his last interview, given during his fatal illness. Again, it refers obliquely to our student discussions over our drafts, by beginning and ending with 'grass' – a joke about minimalism.

He died the same year as Cookson – a double blow.

Almost exactly a year earlier. Their going was, as you say, a double blow. I felt Ian's more because we were then working closely.

Will you write something for William?

There's a depressing story there. Less than three weeks before he died, William rang me up at the last possible moment for getting material into his next issue and pleaded for a poem. He'd actually interrupted me while I was working on an old draft about a remark of his. I promised to send it if I could finish it. That afternoon was the deadline, which I missed. His death twisted it into an elegiac piece. Published first in *The London Magazine* as 'Second Reading', it also appeared, unfortunately with a misprint, in the memorial issue of *Agenda*.

Some of your most highly praised work has been translation, which you say is 'perhaps just as destructive' of your own poetry as reviewing and criticism – and presumably teaching as well. You said, 'There's an awful lot of time looking things up, checking things out.'

The reception of the translations took me by surprise. I'd never intended to carry on after the Villon. Translation can be bad for perpetrator poets, let alone their victims. The psychic energy translation takes differs in several respects from that needed to write poems. The task can become too absorbing, a delaying tactic to put off completing a troublesome poem until the translating is finished. Poets often do it in a dry patch – to 'tide' them over – but it can spread the desert. As many poets have witnessed, to write real poems you need untrammelled vigilance of a strange kind because you don't know what you are on watch for until it finds you. Translation can be used as a sort of respectable distraction and relaxation from this. The risk for poets who don't translate is of filling the watching and waiting time with verse rather than poems. So it's a toss-up who comes off best in the end.

Still, it seems unfair that good poets can be left as blank books to monoglots, so I feel an obligation to get it as right and as complete as I can for source-poet and reader. Untranslated, or badly translated, foreign poets are like Ariel trapped in the tree-trunk of their own language when they should be on paper anywhere. Contrary to much contemporary assumption and presumption, the greatest poetry may well be the sort that survives in translation – if the translation is good enough.

Recently you've been working on a fifth 'corrected' edition of your Dante translation.

Yes, it came out in autumn 2004.

What is it that's been corrected?

Translation never finishes. So, apart from the odd slip and typo, various words and lines that still niggle me are being improved, I hope. Improvements can become a chore because of the running rhyme. Changing or moving a rhyme, if you have to accommodate another correction, may involve rejigging from three to nine lines. It can feel as if you've merely moved a compromise several lines further forward or back.

You began your translation as the result of a 'thwarted reading' while writing your book on rhyme technique. Can you tell us more about this?

William Cookson had republished the Binyon terza rima version – largely, I think, because Pound had praised it. But I was not impressed with it. I thought Pound had praised it partly for personal reasons and partly to boost Dante in the Anglo-Saxon world, not for any genuinely deep critical reason. There wasn't much versified Dante about when Binyon did it. The Dent Temple Classics edition was the popular, influential prose crib, and the Cary, done in the nineteenth century, tended to be the staple blank-verse version. Yet Binyon and then Sayers showed it might be done in rhyme. So my interest in the problem grew, under my skin, from there on.

In preparing the book on rhyme, I looked again at the openings of Sayers, Binyon, and several others. Being about to criticize them in print, I felt that in all fairness I ought to put my head on the opening line and try. But the *b* rhyme in each tercet leaps forward and only stops leaping at the end of a canto, so that was where I had to get in order to excuse myself – at least to myself. An old literary friend was impressed enough with this hasty canto to persuade me to keep at it. The rhyme book got put on the back burner and eventually came out after the Dante.

At the time you began, you had no Italian, let alone medieval Italian. So how did you proceed with the translation? How long did it take?

Very gingerly, over a long time – ten years, in fact – to reach a continuous readable copy. Then it was delayed with a Canadian publisher for years. Peter Jay at Anvil took it over and it was revised again before he published it.

The process was one I don't usually follow when translating. This time I consulted the critical books, annotated editions of the scholars, and various language books first, and decided never to look further at any versified versions until I had a tolerable complete draft of the poem. The Italian I learned in the process is a book Italian. Education in languages during my school and college years was dominated by literature and the page, not by speech, tourism and business, so I was used to the process. Unfortunately, learning languages late in life means that they're no more permanent in the mind than a file on a floppy.

After a day's teaching and half an evening on department work, I'd turn to the *Commedia* and would not go to bed till I'd made a rhymed draft of one canto. The first clumsy complete rhymed draft was made in just over a hundred days – well, evenings.

One canto a night! But you said just now you went slowly and gingerly!

I did slow down once I knew it could be rhymed fairly sensibly. I had to be sure of that before committing precious spare time to it. Initial tinkering began on the weekends as I typed up the week's versions. I tend to become tunnel-visioned when working on something. The *Paradiso* was done before *Purgatorio* because I thought that would force me to join them up by doing the middle bit. Longfellow seems to have worked backwards from the *Paradiso*.

Few others have tackled a terza rima translation, aside from Binyon – to my recollection, only Dorothy Sayers has tried. I notice you don't mention her attempt in your introduction; it's not well-regarded nowadays. Could you comment a little on the previous translations? You wrote: 'every version I had tried to read ... irritated me in similar ways.'

Literary translation has few rewards, so the introduction doesn't pick on any individual writers in making points. Some general readers find Dorothy Sayers's version easier reading than Binyon's. But the rhymes, diction, and syntax of both tend to distract me. On the other hand, Sayers' notes are very interesting and Binyon gave me the bug. He also showed that Dante made a great deal of sense even when not festooned with notes.

Dante is much simpler in style than nearly all of the English translations manage to be. My recent work of revising has been more concerned with syntax and lucidity than the mere rhyme caper. Dante's sweet new style is not always what you could call sweet and simple. No translator risks the full flavour of what Dante occasionally does, and seems to like doing:

> s'io m'*intuassi*, come tu t'*inmii*.

Literally something like, 'if I could self-in-be you as you self-in-be me'. I was going to imitate that sort of thing but finally decided against it. Such oddities would have needed footnotes for general readers and I wanted an approachable, single-volume Dante. It occurs to me that perhaps that line might be a wishful epigraph to my own stuff.

Lowell wrote that 'Strict metrical translators ... are taxidermists, not poets, and their poems are likely to be stuffed birds.'

Lowell's remarks were dealt with in the introduction to my version of Villon published by Penguin, 1978: 'It seems to me that to translate a very formal poet into free verse is as odd as to attempt to translate *The Cantos* into heroic couplets.' Perhaps it would have been clearer to have said alexandrine couplets, as if into French – though someone early on did propose putting *Paradise Lost* into couplets. Strict metrical versions are – like rhyme in general – good or bad depending on who does them and to whom. There's no Law of the Medes and Persians that they have to be stuffed and dead. He 'stuffed' some of his translations with Lowell.

You've been attracted to terza rima in your own poetry – for example, in the 'Mirrors, Windows' and 'Like a Vow' sequences. It's an unusual taste for an English writer. Was it inspired by a long familiarity with Dante? Or did writing in terza rima deepen your connection to him enough to intrigue you with a translation?

It wasn't inspired by him initially. The early attempts derived from British experience: Empson had done some; MacNeice wrote a lot of terza rima. I knew 'Little Gidding', of course. It wasn't the form that drew me to Dante, but after doing him I was interested in the eleven-syllable line and rhyme with light endings, so I tried it out in various forms in *Like a Vow*. In *Mirrors, Windows*, I used it to update Shelley's terza-rima sonnet-form used in 'Ode to the West Wind'. Frost's terza rima sonnet 'Acquainted with the Night' has always been in my head.

Poet-critic Adam Kirsch wrote recently in Slate *magazine that we live in a 'golden age of Dante translation', pointing out that in the last year alone five new editions of the* Inferno *have been published – that's including a reprint of the landmark Longfellow translation, but not including the highly touted 1995 Robert Pinsky translation – and three new translations of the* Inferno. *Why the sudden interest in Dante? Any theories?*

Well, my suspicion is that the millennium had something to do with it: the seven-hundredth year after the notional date of the *Commedia*. Binyon, Eliot, Pound, Heaney and many others have all contributed to contemporary poets' awareness of Dante as a major poet. The Formalist school in America would have to be interested, wouldn't you think? I suspect too that the rise of Islamic fundamentalism has made many people in the West look again at Christianity and, let's face it, Catholicism looks more of a bulwark against anything than would a dry-stone wall of variously shaped Protestant sects.

You comment that Pound's interest in Dante is eccentric, since he conceives of a Dante more or less without Dante's religion. Similarly, Kirsch commented that the current interest in Dante is also partial: Seamus Heaney looks at the way Dante combines the political and the transcendent, which reflects his own Northern Irish perspective, Merwin sees the way Dante uses poets as teachers and role models, etc. Is this simply a modern problem, or have all ages seen Dante so partially?

Wasn't it Frank Kermode who proposed as part of the definition of a classic that each age could bring, or take away from one, its own interpretation? In the 'Introduction' to my Dante, I quoted C. H. Sisson, who suggested that translation is a similar sort of siphoning off of what a period can take from the original text. All translation, of course, is a species of interpretation and criticism. We all see the world partially. Homer, Shakespeare and Dante offer us worlds.

Kirsch comments on the popularity of the Inferno, *saying that 'only hell seems less like fiction than history'. Do you agree? Certainly that would account for the apparent lack of interest in the* Paradiso*! Why is that sublime and fascinating work so much less regarded and translated?*

Punishment, pain, penitence – most humans have experience of these things that dominate the first two parts of the poem. But bliss that increases by whirling faster and shining brighter seems a fairly abstract idea of the joyousness of heaven. Dante's visual and embodying skills make you feel you are 'there' in the first two parts, but you seldom feel that in the third for more than moments. The willing suspension of disbelief doesn't, can't happen there. In some ways the Garden of Eden descriptions in Purgatory can be felt as more blissful after all the previous struggles than Heaven seems, but there are many compensating virtues in the third part. The *Paradiso* may be underrated. Some readers prefer *Hamlet* to *Lear*. Is it literary judgement or personal proclivity?

You didn't know much Italian when you began your translation of the Commedia, *but I'm pretty certain you had no familiarity at all with Tamil when you began your translations from that language. How did your attraction to the language and its poetry begin?*

My then-agent sent me Kokilam Subbiah's notes and prose versions and enquired whether I could turn them into anything viable. I used to meet her to work through the texts. She left for Chicago when we were halfway through, if I remember rightly. That gave me a freer hand.
    The dialogue/duologue aspect attracted me and the interest of a very different tradition of verse. You're quite right, though: I knew nothing of Tamil, classical or current, as a language.

You say you acquired a 'book Italian' translating Dante. How much Tamil did you manage to learn along the way?

I learnt a bit about how it would sound. Later I mugged up a lot more on classical Tamil prosody, which I had ignored in my versions – and read in translation some of the longer poems. Fascinating as it is, I did not succeed in approaching any English 'equivalence' to the prosody for the further Cankam poems I did in the Nineties. I know next to nothing of the language outside that.

It's not fashionable nowadays to link the life with the art, but certainly

Villon's life and the subject matter of his poetry have been unappealing to many, despite the artistry, which is often not readily accessible to English speakers. He's attracted some gifted poets as translators, as varied as Galway Kinnell and Richard Wilbur. But what attracted you to begin your own highly praised translations of Villon?

That's another William story. Quoting Pound on Villon's succinctness in rhyming, one night in the pub, he said Villon was impossible to translate because he always rhymed on the exact word. I bet him it could be done and set out to do it. No money ever changed hands, so I still don't know who won the bet. Having started I became absorbed. A version of the mystery of the connection, the gelling, between translator and source poet, I put in the Anvil edition's 'Preamble'. His humour, realism and quick reversals of emotional direction were fascinating and hooked me. Dante was in a way the last medievalist trying to squeeze the essence of his individual thought into the old prevailing authoritarian wisdom, whereas Villon was in some ways the first modern in spreading doubt about, casting aspersions on, and mocking the Aristotelian and schoolmen's ways of thought. In broad terms, he was a system-wrecking feeler rather than a system-straining thinker. But Villon gets under the skin in some mysterious way.

I was impressed with the immediacy and energy of your translations.

Occasionally I had the eerie impression that Villon nagged at me in the night to improve some rhyme or pun, or make some refinement. I'd get up and jot it down. 'Villon, the dead man, speaks with me,' I said in that 'Preamble'. That kind of absorption perhaps contributes to the immediacy of the version.

Villon nagged at you in the night? That throws a whole different light on Auden's comment about the arts being our only means of communication with the dead!

It's just that you have made an English voice for him and you get so wrapped up in speaking in it that the brain must go on to auto-pilot in the night. I'm a bit of an insomniac. You spend quite a time wondering whether the verse will stay put till morning and reluctantly decide you have to get up and jot it down.

Donald Davie criticized you a bit for cramping Villon's lines into shorter meters, but, in my own humble verse translations from the French, that's almost impossible not to do, isn't it?

You're right; you usually need to do that. As far as I remember, Davie was referring to the 'Ballade and Prayer' written for Villon's mother, and the first version of the 'Ballade of the Men Hanged'. I took his advice and went for a longer line in revising the Penguin edition for Anvil. After all, logically, if I had once shortened the line in those two, the rest of the body of the text would have to be in trimeters. But you need space for joking and punning.

Perhaps that's why you don't 'emasculate' Villon, as Davie maintains Swinburne and Rossetti do. Nothing emasculates more than excess baggage.

I agree. It may be because I brought many traditional blank-verse procedures into the tetrameter arena. Nabokov's *Notes on Prosody* gave me one or two useful ideas. But it's interesting how period concerns in poetry get into those translations of theirs.

Can you give an example or two?

Well, off the top of my head: thou-ing and thee-ing, the odd Miltonic straddle of adjectives across nouns, 'tis and 'twas, the relative clause distant from its antecedent ...
    They get into ours but we are too close to see most of them clearly. A small example: in the early translation, at the end of the liberated Sixties, I used 'fuck' in the 'Ballade of Fat Margot'. At that time, dozens of authors were trying to liberate such swearwords into print – a passing bravado. Macmillan wrapped the entire volume in cellophane to keep themselves unsullied. Sexual terms in French and English never quite match, so it is a problem. Later I took it out.
    There's a dramatic strand to translating; you're trying to create the voice and mannerisms of the character of a foreign text. That's what you have to convey – the voice that speaks believably.

I always find that a concise English translation from the French leaves you an extra foot or two. David Cooke also criticizes Lowell for excessive pruning, and he is at the opposite end of the spectrum from you.

Yes, I usually shorten the French line, too. But I often feel that Lowell turned his sources into versions of Lowell. I've always tried to keep out of my versions as far as is possible.

Do you ever spot Peter Dale creeping in, regardless?

I'm probably the last person to be able to detect that. The first version of Villon was printed with lower-case line-openings, but then I thought that was too much my own preference in verse-layout so it was printed as normal verse in later texts.

But it was the formal challenge that attracted you to the project, originally?

That was one of the things – the challenge William set me to win. Villon's stanza rhymes *ababbcbc*, requiring four matching rhymes and two pairs per verse. In pure-rhyme in English this can be a tall order if you also want the pace, puns, wit, and succinctness. If you're an ambitious tightrope walker, Niagara Falls always beckons. Metrical translation's a bit like hanging in the morning: it clarifies the mind.

Perhaps that's the best reply to Lowell's 'stuffed birds'! Is your mind clarified of translating now; did it work?

I keep saying to myself, right, this is the last time, the last translation ... but there's a bilingual version of Corbière's *Les Amours jaunes* just appearing and I'm on the verge of polishing off a version of Valéry's *Charmes*. So I'll tell myself again: no more.

Even after hearing that your Corbière has just been announced as the Poetry Book Society's Recommended translation for the quarter?

Well, it might tempt me to keep adding to a random collection of one-off translations that has built up over the years, but Valéry, I think, will be my last bookful.

Maybe we could go back, for a moment, to Lowell: in your Lowell and Berryman review, you commented that the poet is 'the most unpoetical thing on earth'.

Yes, Keats again.

You were quarrelling, I believe, with a whole spate of writers writing about writing. I don't blame you, but you would be an odd fish if you didn't succumb to that temptation, too. Have you?

Occasionally. I try not to. With poems dedicated to writer friends you can hardly avoid touching on some issues. My biggest *mea culpa* would be 'Summer Shadows', one of the few poems of mine which is, on one level, about writing as writing.

Oh, but it's so very gently about writing, compared with the worst offenders. There's a lot of grandstanding and posturing out there! After you read an anthology some years ago, you commented: 'Then I remember being irritated by the number of poems in it that mentioned words like 'poem,' 'poet,' 'writer,' 'verse'. It seemed to me arid, navel-gazing.'

All of the arts are built on various conventions and 'as ifs'. We watch plays as if they are reality. Poetry has similar conventions. In some ways, it's the most intimate of the arts. J. S. Mill, among others, including Eliot, suggests that poems are eavesdropped: 'we should say that eloquence is heard, poetry is overheard. Eloquence supposes an audience; the peculiarity of poetry appears to us to lie in the poet's utter unconsciousness of a listener. All poetry is of the nature of soliloquy.'

In lyric, poets frequently write in the second person singular form in intimate close-up, but the poem has to give the impression that it's unaware of a reader eavesdropping the conversation and the reader must feel invisible. If you introduce words and ideas about writing the stuff, both poet and reader become uneasily aware and self-conscious about being where they are, doing what they're doing. The best poetry aims to strike at a deeper level than self-consciousness. The problem is, in a way, approached from an odd angle, perhaps, in the poem 'Against Superstition'.

There are no rules about it. 'Was it the proud full sail of his great verse?' That anthology and that period were too full of it – people chasing around the same houses, attitudinizing about poets and poems. There's just far too much of that in the twentieth century and on. It's a dead genre.

You've said, 'And as you get older this problem looms larger, in my opinion. You cannot predict the kind of poems that are going to impress and move you. They come in surprising places.' Why does this problem get larger as you get older, in your opinion?

Judgement about anything and everything gets harder as you get older.

Well yes, youth is so hard on everything, and I find young reviewers can be so much less sympathetic than older ones.

You're right there. Well, the number of 'poems' is constantly increasing. You meet new poems and have a longer perspective to see them from. You've seen poems that were praised to the skies during your youth now come down to earth. You read ones that successfully ignore the critical tenets that surrounded you then. You change. Another aspect may be that you remember that period of committed youth and would like to think that it was poetically acute and not just inexperienced, hard and intemperate. So there's an insidious nostalgia for youth and certainty, which paradoxically leads to more hesitation. There are poems best appreciated by youth and, obviously, others best appreciated by age, experience and retrospection. Yet hesitant age may be as misguided as intemperate youth.

How easy to call a poem bad!

Yes, well, the odds are on it; there are more bad than good. But it's just as easy for some to call a poem good. Critics can be glib and baffling in either direction. Some judges are trustworthy or at least understandable. Others are not.

Looking back over the years, what kinds of poems have taken you by surprise – can you think of the most memorable examples?

Larkin's free, or free-ish, verse, surprised me: 'Coming', 'Going' and 'If, my Darling', in particular. It's surprising he didn't write more. He said in a letter that Laforgue's free-verse 'The Coming Winter', from the *Last Poems*, was a poem he'd been trying to write all his life. Thom Gunn's 'The Feel of Hands' was so good it made me look again at the idea of syllabics. Hill is always surprising: the prose poems of *Mercian Hymns*, the almost 'straight', certainly strait, lyrics in *The Songbook of Sebastian Arrurruz*, the formal power of *The Mystery of the Charity of Charles Péguy*. Muldoon's 'Incantata' also took me by surprise – a poet who I thought had more talent than he knew what to do with. I've never been fond of heavily repeating forms but my first encounter with Corbière's *Rondels* for *After* bowled me over. Roethke's 'The Lost Son' impressed me at college. Hecht's 'Rites and Ceremonies' also made an indelible impression. I'd always been impressed by 'The Vow' and 'Adam' which I'd known earlier, but this was moving wider.

You and Ian Hamilton refer to 'Kleenex poems' – that is, disposable poetry, in Hamilton's words. You say, 'Yes, well it used to be called 'verse' in the old days, that disposable stuff. A distinction used to be maintained. In the modern period it's been confused.' Do you find that there's pressure to make poetry into mere entertainment? America's 'poetry slams' come to mind – as well as a few prominent poets I shan't name.

To some extent. Auden was right to insist that poetry should contain the whole spectrum of life. Currently the number of colours may have been reduced. I hesitate these days to read quite a few of my poems in public readings. Modern audiences don't seem to want to take straight the old themes, heart-cry, birth and copulation and death, *lachrimae rerum* and so forth. – And academics prefer poetry they need to explicate. – But to be fair, I find it hard to read *Da Capo* even to myself – if I ever have to. It makes me feel suicidal at the sheer inconsequence of humanity and its relationships. Why should an audience *pay* to experience any of that? You don't really know what an audience is after. You just have to write the poems that demand to be written.

Incidentally, Frost gave an amusing analysis of audiences at readings. It's cited by Burnshaw in *Robert Frost Himself*: 'Do you still divide your audiences into halves, as you told Louis [Untermeyer]? ... half likers, half haters; then cut each half into quarters – one for the wrong, one for the right reasons?'

I recall Colin Falck's remarks: 'Poetry may have lost some of its pretentiousness in recent years but it has also lost the greater part of its ambition.' That was written in the early Seventies, but thirty years later, it still seems to be true.

Hughes and Hill seem to have big ambitions. Falck was speaking, I think, of the so-called Movement and its wake. But poetry isn't a single psyche with one ambition and never was. It lost its audience – the audience that Byron and Tennyson chiefly had greatly extended – when it became estranged by aspects of modernism. Its confinement in the ghetto of academic specialization and the proliferation of alternative modern media also helped diminish its general influence. (Some cynics say its decline began when English Literature became a respectable academic subject with its own specialists.) In the Sixties, many thought the answer was to compromise with populism and performance, going for a musicless pop-music. The claims of poetry may have become like those of the three London bakers in one street: the first advertises: *Best baker in London*; the second: *Best baker in England*; the third: *Best baker in this street*. Well, there may only be a street but the poetry in it might as well be the best in the street. The trouble is that home-baking machines have also come in.

You yourself have been associated by some with a movement – the so-called 'Review Group,' which included Ian Hamilton, David Harsent, Hugo Williams, Colin Falck, you and others. 'Real' poets tend to view these kinds of movements as marketing gimmicks – more beloved of critics and publishers than the poets themselves. But can you describe any common ground for this one?

I was tangential to most of that, never having been a joiner. Like all young groups it arose out of irritation with immediate forebears, tended to think the Movement was in a rut of irony and caution, a formal lack of risk, but it didn't want to skip back to the bardic bogusness of Dylan Thomas. Authentic feeling was the issue, feeling things on the pulses, rather than in armoured gauntlets of irony. (Corbière wrote: I have taken life off with my gloves.) The Review group wanted a more lived-in poetry rather than excogitated verse.

Early Pound and imagism seemed to offer possibilities of developments. I said I was tangential just now; that was also because I didn't think that an adaptation of imagism necessarily required free verse and extreme brevity – minimalism. Ian was the controlling force behind the group and the kind of poetry he was after at that time seemed restricted to a fairly narrow spectrum. I found a more independent range for experiment in working with *Agenda*. Ian was going to do one of those small *Review* pamphlets of my poems but by then I had placed *The Storms* with Macmillan, and had nothing much else available. All of us, except Ian and Michael Fried, developed rapidly away from those beginnings. It was a short-lived movement. Ian spoke of its heyday as 1963-68, minimal itself. Michael Fried's one-liners signalled the extreme limit and limitations – the end of the line, you might say.

You've said, 'But poetry may be one activity where practice doesn't make perfect.' But it does help, surely? Is poetry different from any of the other arts in this regard? After all, practising piano lots won't make you Alfred Brendel, but it does give you technical precision.

Poetry may be different. After all, execution is not quite original creation. Technical precision and practice help you to write verse or verses. Poetry is a bit more complicated. Remember Browning's perfect painter Andrea del Sarto:

> That arm is wrongly put ...
> ... and I could alter it
> But all the play, the insight and the stretch –
> Out of me, out of me.

Practice can often be the reiteration of the methods used for previous poems and this kind of repetition towards facility may slow or prevent a breakthrough or move forward. Someone said Auden had such facility that he had in later years to introduce increasing technical difficulty in new work. He did weird things like combining alcaics with Welsh englyn.

In which poems?

The englyn/alcaics are in *Streams*; another englyn is *In Memoriam L. K.-A.* He was always seeking complex forms to try – like Portuguese *cantiga*, admittedly in a nonsense poem, *Nursery Rhyme*, which makes it easier.
  Eliot is probably in agreement about 'practising', when he says in 'East Coker':

> Because one has only learnt to get the better of words
> For the thing one no longer has to say ...

Perhaps I'm quarrelling with the mainstream view that, when it comes to poetry, feeling and thought is everything, with technical skill a distant subordinate. The dangers of technical facility you are discussing are so far, far beyond most of what you see in poetry journals nowadays.

Well, Horace put it succinctly years ago: art is the art of concealing art. The trouble with so-called spontaneous expression is that artlessness is all you get. Spontaneity is the end-product of good composition, not necessarily the starting point. (Look how Beethoven struggled in his notebooks.) Authenticity might be the better word. But it's a more or less permanent problem. To some extent, good as his ear was, Pound's complaint against the pentameter was caused by a lack of understanding of how the British wrote and read it, and the variability in the weight of stress and expression that it allowed. Frost was much more on the ball there. As for the skills required for poems, Valéry said that poets work *with* the difficulty of language, not *against* it. Coleridge spoke of a poem containing: 'a more than usual state of emotion, with more than usual order' – which sums up the formal position in a nutshell. A spring produces most tension when fixed at both ends and compressed.

You've dismissed syllabics as incompetence – although you qualified that a bit earlier with your comments on Gunn's 'The Feel of Hands' – and defended the metrical line at a time when it's been under fire. Yet you are a free-verse poet as well. Wyatt Prunty said that you are 'poised between the traditionalist's respect for meter and rhyme and the revolutionary's conviction that only freedom produces authenticity.' Is that a fair summation of your position?

Yes. I've edged away from that early position on syllabics a bit. I'm still against mere counting, but Auden and Gunn have combined syllabics with the metrical tradition and even with stress-verse, and the mix can be very effective. I've been developing a syllabic system recently based on the caesura, a bit like traditional French methods, rather than counting to line-ends. I've also experimented with what I call cadence syllabics, which involve stress. This is caesural:

> Where have you gone,|| Eurydice,| oh, my love
> of life?|| Where have you fled? || In the dark,
> the music casts no light;|| my hands lie dumb.||
> The pipes are broken and cracked the harp.||
> Eurydice,|| what music can be strung
> on dry sticks?|| I'll find my voice.|| I'll bring you,|
> wherever you are held, ||a song of love.||
> It will marmorealise all Dis||
> to set you free.|| Orpheus, | the singer,|
> swears you this.

Not my usual subject matter, but this experiment is based on a syllable count of four before the caesura and nine after it. The two counts vary widely, so that in the count of nine, subsidiary pauses may occur to prevent everything being too rigid and obvious. It is combined with a fairly iambic base rhythm and various rhyme types. The double stroke indicates the count; the single the subsidiary pauses.

Metre's just a tool – no more compulsory than rhyme. A poet needs to understand and use it to establish authentic personal rhythms.

How?

Well, Shakespeare's pentameters are different from Pope's or Milton's in the types of variability of foot and weight of stress each of them uses, the kinds of things they permit at the caesura, with the caesura and line-end, the type of sound-effects they prefer. And they differ from Wordsworth's and Tennyson's, Hill's, Stevens's, Frost's and Larkin's. Despite these personal habituations, it is clear they are all using a similar metrical basis for the line.

Free verse is just another set of forms that need to be done skilfully. Shelley said: 'Every great poet must inevitably innovate upon the example of his predecessors in the exact structure of his peculiar versification.' I assume he's using 'peculiar' in the Authorized Version meaning of 'individual' or 'personal'. Convincing rhythm is what a good poet turns metrics into.

Of course the whole debate – free vs. formal verse – burned much hotter in the U.S. than it did in the U.K. Has the whole argument become boring?

Yes. It's a pseudo-revolution that's been coming round every generation or so since about 'Dover Beach'. George Herbert, a superb metrist, wrote one free-verse poem in 'The Collar'. What's new? Karl Shapiro, not one of my favourite poets, perhaps got it right when he wrote: '"Iambic pentameter" represented the poetry of English rhythm for a thousand years. This was not "ritual"; it was "the poetry of" the rhythm of our language. The situation in America demanded a new rhythm which we are still trying to find.' The remark would be more accurate, perhaps, if one removed the word 'pentameter'.

Maybe that search is the problem. If, for example, you take the spread of American pronunciations like 'tèmporárily', America may be moving towards iambic more so than the old British 'témporarily', which verges on paeonic, a stress followed by three light syllables that the end is often reduced to here.

In your satire, 'The New Testament of Jean de Calais', you wrote: 'men ought to write what they can speak.' William Bedford once described a conflict in your work between 'narrative demands and poetic intensity'. He said that some time ago, and you've managed to resolve that riddle since then, certainly by the time you wrote One Another. *How?*

That line you quote was about Pound's and other modernists' playing around with foreign languages, bleeding gobbets. Dudley Fitts had always to check Pound's classical snippets for the publisher. In secret, I think.

The resolution of the riddle came from doing *The Seasons of Cankam*. I looked again at free verse and the whole idea of dialogue and duologue. The first result was the sequence called *The Going*. Mandelstam said 'There is no lyric without dialogue.'

It's a taste that seems to have served you well, with One Another, *then* Mirrors, Windows, *and* Da Capo.

Yes, well the English poet C. H. Sisson once wrote – where I forget – that two is the least number of minds an intelligent person can be in. The dramatic approach to lyric allows for this and a bit more if necessary.

Your later poems have of course been praised precisely for the lyric intensity they bring to very quiet, often domestic, moments. Terry Eagleton wrote in 1970 that your challenge was overcoming an 'occasional thinness of experience, for which honesty of feeling seemed at times frail compensation', and spoke of your 'sliding into laconic flatness ... an unduly repressive reticence'. What changed for you, and in you? Keeping in mind your claim that practice doesn't make perfect in poetry!

I junked my well-practised methods. After that experience with *Cankam*, I began to think of lines more as contour lines. There may be flattish ones and winding, twisting ones, variously close together or variously spaced, the odd doubling back almost, to show the eventual heights.

An example of what you mean would be helpful.

One Another is the most complex example, perhaps, as sonnets and styles reflect, contrast and recapitulate in different ways and sometimes on different readings. In *Da Capo*, when the reader gets to 'Envoy', many of the previous lines need doubling back on – that is, they will need re-reading, and the preceding and succeeding context will then need reconsiderations that spread like rings in water. To give a different, rather clunking example from a mini-sequence, look at the syntax and registers in the sonnet 'Platonic' in *Edge to Edge*. The variation of the caesura and the stopping, the puns, the lyric interlude of 'Dream easier to chase, death easier to lay', the collision of particle physics, Latin and the Elizabethan conjuring pun – it all adds up to a very feisty female. 'This birch I touch into your memories.' What sort of touch, what sort of birch? The form is almost breaking with her fury.

PLATONIC

You never raped my soul – and that is why
I hate you. Everything you thought you'd had:
my little finger, lips, my barefoot pad,
tilt of the head, fishnet across a thigh,
as if these held in truth the very thing.
And the old burrow to the familiar dark,
your knick-knack cyclotron to hold that spark
in vacuo by conjuring in the ring!

Your soul, poor stump, has never made my soul.
But mine would soon have shown you what rape is,
if you were of my kind, near my black hole.
– Dream easier to chase, death easier to lay,
than going round this corner where I turn away.
This birch I touch into your memories.

Look at fishnet, thing, stump, black hole. What sort of fish in what peculiar river? The black hole turns 'voidlet' in the next sonnet. My little finger – round which you wind people. The next two sonnets develop many of these images and rhythms. The rush of words is splashing thoughts and ideas about.

It depends on speech rhythms woven in and out of metrics like that, and, as Frost puts it, sentence sounds. One sentence sound, simple statement, contrasting, combining with other types, like contours from which a map-reader can imaginatively walk the gradients and reach the point from which the whole view strikes home. Burnshaw's *The Seamless Web* has a good chapter touching on the different types of language that can be subsumed in a single poem.

In addition, *Cankam* had a sort of established set of meanings or implications for different types of landscape.

Can you give some examples of what you mean by that?

Well, the landscapes are associated with types of culture: the shore with fishing; the jungle with hunting; arable lands with farming; deserts with banditry ... The plants of these areas could become shorthand for types of person or moods, and the seasons could be added in for the ups and downs of love relationships. That, too, had an influence on me, moving me towards the greater emotional concision and shorthand of *One Another*. Hardy does something similar with his spring versus autumn love poems. There's a succinct summary of this and more in the 'Afterword' of A. K. Ramanujan's book of translations, *The Interior Landscape*, Peter Owen, published way back in 1970.

You've been said to have a high 'meaning-to-words ratio', and your work would certainly be found quite difficult by the person with a taste for 'Kleenex poetry'.

One has to write to last and, as we said earlier, literature should invite renewed reading and should reward the effort more than once or twice. There are people who read Jane Austen and other classics annually. The works of art I like are those based in concentrations, essences: lyric and dramatic as opposed to narrative and epic, miniatures, not murals. I remember an art critic, in discussing on television a miniature painting, saying of it that, small as it was, the background was still monumental in effect. It would be great if you could get that into a lyric. Which reminds me of something Geoffrey Hill wrote, expounding an idea of Simone Weil's: 'lyric poetry is necessarily dramatic: indeed, the "different planes" actually available to a director on his theatre-stage could even be regarded as an indication of what takes place "simultaneously" in the arena of the poem.' ('The Conscious Mind's Intelligible Structure', *Agenda* 9.4-10.1)

While some have praised your 'use of language at a minimal level of syntactic complexity' – that comes from Stephen Wade — others have explored the ambiguity of your use of certain words and phrases. W.G. Shepherd singles out this one, so I will too, from 'Upland' – 'I find you many likely places.' Which of course has the double meaning of 'I find many likely places for you' and 'I find you in many likely places.'

I didn't put that 'in' there. So whose ambiguity is it? Ambivalent levels of expression are a device I use where necessary, and only occasionally, as do many other poets. Hill, for example: 'Innocence is no earthly weapon.' Or Shakespeare: 'The expense of spirit in a waste of shame'. It's sometimes essential. 'Odi et amo,' as Catullus wrote. In poems you can sometimes get conflicting feelings like that into one word well placed or into one line. We are not always sure of what we feel: 'Dark promises, my love, lie candid there.' Or how about this for a rejection slip: 'We have read your work and much like it.'?

'Stopping by Woods on a Snowy Evening' is wonderfully simple but operates on at least two levels. As for simple vocabulary and syntax, could you cram any more into 'Neither out Far Nor in Deep' with a Miltonic syntax or Cantos-like gobbets? Trilling said at Frost's eighty-fifth celebrations that it was a poem 'that often seems to me the most perfect poem of our time'.

You've spoken elsewhere about the perils of using a 'conversational style', and that you are after a 'natural style', rather than a 'conversational' one that changes from year to year, place to place.

And sometimes poem to poem. But it's not so much the *perils* of a conversational style as the possible *limitations*. It is, of course, the natural style for some genres of verse. Yet in ordinary conversation certain words sound pretentious, like name-dropping, or sudden bursts of French or what have you. (Look back at '*in vacuo*'. It's justified by the furious irony, not by some law of conversational style.) Wilde has superb examples of using pretentious words in conversation for his own comic effects: 'rise, sir, from that semi-recumbent position', and so forth. But for certain effects or ideas a poet or writer may need to use any of these things, and words not generally regarded as conversationally current. The currency of speech is quickly devalued as generations and idioms change. The language has to sound right and natural for the dramatic and lyrical situation. We all say extraordinarily odd things in the heat of the moment or emotion. Love-names between couples and among families are extraordinarily odd. Most could not easily be used in a poem. They have to be adapted, as does much else. Coleridge speaks of not imposing an act of uniformity upon poets. So, no absolute laws on diction; perhaps a few rules of thumb about general archaism and the old poetic diction – breakable in an emergency. Emily Dickinson rightly pointed out that the pen has many inflections while the voice has only one at a time.

I want to go back to your 'Not Another Dedication' to Ian Hamilton, where you cite his words, 'The imaginable moral power ... of perfect speech'. Undoubtedly, your understanding of what he meant expresses something that meant a lot to both of you.

I suppose it might. We never discussed the phrase – my use of it – or how it might relate to our own writing. My understanding of what he meant may by now be skewed. Over the years I've probably misapplied it in a sort of talismanic way. The phrase is from his Lowell biography. Referring to *Life Studies*, he sums up: '... his one remaining faith, if one can call it that, is in the imaginable moral power of perfect speech.' Previously in the biography Ian's unease with the apocalyptic religiose moral stance along with the thumping iambics of early Lowell is apparent. Ian characterizes the poems now as acknowledging that poetry makes nothing happen but they seek 'to be refreshed by a direct, almost wide-eyed attentiveness to objects, places, personal experience.' – Of course, Ian and I discussed such things together but not in terms of the quotation used in 'Not Another Dedication'.

Shelley wrote: 'The great instrument of moral good is the imagination.' Ian is showing his usual canniness and critical caution: 'imaginable' allows for a possible moral power in the art to be an ideal a little firmer than 'imaginary', and of course perfect speech is rarely to be had in natural languages and live situations; it is another ideal for poems. You just have to feel that if you could capture the poem perfectly in words it would necessarily have some sort of power for good. This steers clear of asserting simply a direct moral function for poetry because it gives imagination its role. (Presumably the reader does the imaginable bit, too.) Second, the emphasis is on perfecting the utterance, the spell of the poem, to make it work. That imaginative conviction, however passing, seems essential. Making a poem is such a complex, absorbing, vital experience that you feel it must do something if only you can get it right. Without ideals like those, most poets would, or should, stop writing. You have to believe somehow that it is worth doing, that it eventually makes a difference. Geoffrey Hill once said in an interview with John Haffenden: 'Poetry is responsible. It's a form of responsible behaviour, not a directive. It is an exemplary exercise.' We're speaking here of the attempt to write poetry, of course, not verse.

In the article 'The New Freedom of Rhyme', you describe the great variety of vowel and consonant repetition that has come into use since Owen's pararhyme. You've certainly supported that argument with your superb book, An Introduction to Rhyme *– I don't know of a better one on the subject. You've been called one of the subtlest rhymers in English since*

Emily Dickinson. It's not an entirely fashionable taste in an era that has favoured free verse.

I don't see her as consciously experimental in rhyme; she was more often an impatient rhymer in the heat of composition.

Fashion pundits often get it wrong. The twentieth century was the biggest period of experiment in rhyme in history. Look at how much blank verse dominates the nineteenth. Yeats, Owen, Frost, Auden, MacNeice, Ransom, Arlington Robinson, Dylan Thomas, Larkin, Hill, Lowell, Wilbur, Hecht, Snodgrass, Muldoon (to cite in any old order) are all masters of rhyme, and in the lyrical work of most of them rhyme of various sorts is commoner than blank and unrhymed verse. Why must we always have to justify it? It's not the essence of poetry, just one of the sounder tools.

Have you had to justify it a lot?

On and off over the years. For a start, as I've said, Ian and I had long friendly debates about it when we were students. He did use quite a bit of rhyme, some slant, in the end. I also remember two American students helping with *Agenda* who rolled about with laughter when William and I were talking of Lowell's metrics and rhyme-methods. They seemed to think he wrote free verse only and that free verse did not rhyme. I've met and argued with British 'poets' with little inkling of the rhythmical and rhyming traditions of English who could not write a practice pentameter if you asked them, let alone a tolerable couplet. On the other hand, there appears to be a feeling in some parts of the English-speaking world now that if a poem is formal it must necessarily be better than if in free verse. It's not the case. Wobbly rhymed, wobbly metrical poems have always been with us.

The curious thing is that the odd typography and lay-outs of, for example, Pound, Cummings and Carlos Williams, seemed to so many critics less odd, less in need of justification than metric or rhyme.

What led you to such an intensive study of the subject of rhyme – through the experiments in your own poetry, and as a scholarly subject for your book?

Well, nursery rhymes, like 'Hey diddle diddle', must have begun it. From an early age I was intrigued by the slight mismatches of rhyme in many of them: 'Lemons/St Clements ... farthings/St Martin's ... pay me/St Bailey'

... 'water/after' ... 'Simon/pie-man' ... 'man/gun'. Of course, I didn't know anything about languages and sound-changes then, but that's where the fascination started. I've always felt the vital importance of some sort of form in art; form pickles the words so that they keep.

I like that! As you've just said, and have also said elsewhere, the twentieth century, and presumably the twenty-first so far, is 'the longest period of experiment in rhyme that there has been.' Well, it's commonly said that English is a rhyme-poor language, perhaps even 'rhymed out'.

Forms may have to lie fallow, as Eliot suggested somewhere, so that they can sprout works with new vigour. Sometimes a great poet more or less commandeers a form, like Pope with the heroic couplet, and if it can't be bettered other things need to develop, like, say, Browning's overrun couplets in 'My Last Duchess'. Languages are seldom rhymed out; their vocabularies are always changing. Periods or individual poets can get jaded over certain forms and again new ways must be found.

New systems of rhyme mean that poets writing English now have much more choice in matching rhyme type to subject, just as the best of them match rhythm to subject. Perhaps the truth is that we live in a period of free rhyme as well as of free verse. The increased experimentation in rhyme may have been a sort of answer-back to the free-versers; even Yeats updated his rhyming methods.

Does this suggest an increasing facility with rhyme – which Milton famously called the 'invention of a barbarous age'?

Yes, rhyme is much easier now that you can choose your method or mix. Milton was partly confusing inflected and uninflected languages and firing at the rhymed-couplet issue that was later to become one of those local period skirmishes in literature – ongoing enough for even the young Keats to get involved. Nobody wants a rhymed *Paradise Lost*. But all of Lowell's unrhymed 'sonnets'?

An obvious question: I notice you tend to avoid pure, or perfect, rhymes – compared to, say, Richard Wilbur. Why?

I don't think I do, though I did ask Wilbur why he seldom tried oblique forms of rhyme. I try to match the type of rhyme to the material. There's a lot of pure rhyme in my work, not just for translations. In *Under the Breath* there are twenty poems in pure rhyme; twenty-three in oblique rhyme; eight in free verse; one in blank verse and one sestina. It's fairly even between pure and oblique rhyme, though the proportions were not consciously planned.

Can you describe a little how you do that – match the type of rhyme to the material?

I wish I could. It must be experience or instinct by now. How do you ride a bike? It's much easier to do than explain. Sometimes verse-form and idea arrive as one and that will often fix the form. Sometimes by its development an idea mutters at you: sestet now, or next verse, or even: wrong form. So I probably phrased the last answer badly: the successful poems choose their form for you and make it apparent fairly early on. It wasn't always like that. 'The Storms' and 'The Fragments', too, started as sonnet sequences; but they seemed uncomfortable that way, and the other forms emerged. But one curiosity that other poets may also have found is that certain forms seem more likely to suggest themselves with this or that poet than other forms do. Variants of the *In Memoriam* stanza, maverick sonnets, versions of terza rima, seem to show up more often than, say, couplets in my mind – as well as stanzas that seem to have invented themselves, as in 'Mottled' or 'Our Place'. Wilbur, I think, mentions his interest in a haiku-like stanza as one of his own forms.

You've also been praised for showing the possibilities of rhyming off the stress or on the first syllable – are we talking about a 'wrenched stress rhyme'?

No, I hate wrenched stress wherever it is. There are three types of what's meant by this off-rhyming. The first, whose technical name is skaldic rhyme, matches the stressed syllable of polysyllables, ignoring the syllables after the stress. Keith Douglas's 'Europe/fury' is an example in his last poem. I'm not sure where he found it but he uses quite a bit of it fairly randomly. There's plenty in MacLeish, Auden, MacNeice – and in Celtic practice. Auden must take the credit for popularizing it as a system. 'Music is International' is a good, showy example. The second type is on-and-off-stress rhyming. Auden's villanelle, 'Miranda', is a wonderful example of that. Marianne Moore used similar devices in her rhymed syllabics, but fairly casually. The third type is light rhyme or rhyme on unstressed syllables only: MacNeice's 'Prognosis' is a fairly dull example. I tried it first, I think, in 'Word' in *Edge to Edge*.

But really, does the ear pick up some of these more esoteric rhymes, or do they tend to become, like syllabics, a rather arbitrary method for disciplining the poet's mind and lines? You described your poem 'Half-Light' as having an unusual abab, cccccc, abab rhyme pattern. In which case, that links as rhymes or near-rhymes: think-chill-instant-windows, night-outside-twice-by, and dance-car-glance-path-glass-past. At least for my ear, some of those are a bit of a stretch. They don't have the effect of rhyme. Am I alone? Or am I missing something?

Well, I can't be sure. I have to trust *my* ear. Assonance is meant to be subtler than full rhyme. The *c* match, long 'ah' in my English, may not work so well in American pronunciation as it does here in Southern England at least. I agree that you might say the two sets of *abab* lines are split too far apart by those *c* rhymes but in each quatrain they have rhyme partners close enough to work; they rhyme, then, as two separate quatrains. Those *c* rhymes bothered me at first, seeming a bit too noisy. As I said before, art is the art of concealing art. Not all effects in the arts are meant to be apprehended consciously. The arts have powers to hit you below that level of attention.

Frost thinks of rhyme as the acoustic equivalent of metaphor – 'the extension of metaphor into sound'. Dick Davis called it the mating of unlike things – like sex. I think Brodsky said pretty much the same – he thought it was part of what made poetry an accelerated mental process. You hint at much the same idea.

Similarly to Dick Davis, Chesterton said the sophisticated pleasure of rhyme was summed up in the fact that *idyll* rhymed with *diddle*. All of those ideas come into it. Laforgue loved to rhyme an elevated word with a low word, to rhyme on near-neologism, 's'enfichent/sandwiche', or to rhyme an airy abstraction with concrete earthiness: 'foetus/Angélus'.

If the sound of a line can have an uncanny effect on the reader, then rhyme-sound is one of the notations that can move the line in the right way. Like Tennyson at his best, and like Owen and Auden, I've tried to use various types of rhyme in order that the rhyme should support the sound structure of the poem more thoroughly than it could in the rather more circumscribed past of pure rhyme. But Stevens can make a wonderful cantabile sound without systematic rhyme and he has been a subterranean influence like Auden.

Brodsky may have a point. Someone once said that Yeats, asked where he got his extraordinary ideas, replied: looking for the next rhyme. And

Dryden – wasn't it? – said that many a time a rhyme had helped him to a thought. Cowper complained that it came uncalled for when he was trying to write blank verse. It affects poets and poems themselves in all sorts of odd ways. If memory serves me right, Valéry said that young poets may be led to a rhyme by an idea and mature poets are oftener led to an idea by a rhyme.

You wrote that rhyme 'is part of the time-capsule that preserves and isolates words in an objective shape that may travel forward through time, changing more slowly than the body – like a sculpture.' Could you make this a little more concrete with an example?

Well, it's not just their obscurity that puts off would-be readers of things like Blake's Prophetic Books. The lack of intelligible form must play some part, among other things. What you've quoted is just an elaboration of Pope's: 'True Art is Nature to advantage dress'd, / What oft was thought but ne'er so well express'd'. Would his satirical points have been so effective and long-lasting in blank or free verse?

We're back to pickling words so that they'll keep, aren't we?

Yes. One special case is interesting, perhaps. How about the Frenchified pronunciation of rhyme in 'They Flee from Me'? That accent and pronunciation is still there though few general readers observe it or preserve it. Although that bit of the language has changed, the moment of the woman's visit has travelled down to us with a living power. The rhyme has preserved the sound, shape and moment. In Wyatt's Chaucerian stanza we still have the diaphanous drape:

> In thin arraye after a pleasaunt gyse,
> When her lose gowne from her shoulders did fall ...

His quirky, individual shaping of the rhythm and form must also have contributed to the poem's long preservation of the moment and feelings. Good free verse can do the same. Free verse *is* allowed to use sound for effect.

You've written two verse plays – Cell and Sephe – albeit several decades ago. It's a somewhat disregarded form, no? In the last century, we've had the verse plays of T.S. Eliot and Christopher Fry – but verse plays have been rather on the downswing in English since Shakespeare.

I've just completed a rewrite of *Sephe*, so I am still at it. I think that *Cell* still works – which means it does what I set out to do. Shortly after completion it was in rehearsal for stage performance, and I saw it work on stage. Unfortunately, the lead actor acquired a good television contract and quit. The period criticism was peremptory. Poets seldom get the run of a theatre to improve their technique, so that's the biggest drawback. Verse plays make all poetry critics jittery and drama critics likewise.

There's been a bit of a resurgence of verse-drama lately, with Tony Harrison, Glyn Maxwell, Sean O'Brien and others here. Wilbur's versions from French seem highly stageable. I've done two more: *The Dark Voyage*, a play for music, now updated from the *Agenda* text, and the latest, unpublished, *The Demiser*, a pale black comedy.

The 1976 play, Cell, *was not one of your more critically successful efforts. In the words of William Bedford, 'Cell fails disastrously, in my opinion, to express the pain that is melodramatically spotlighted...'*

I was not trying to do what he thinks I was attempting.

The play, about a 'political prisoner in an indeterminate modern state', departs from your usual subject matter, which tends to be very much grounded in your own life. Was it your treatment of the subject matter, or the verse play form, that undermined its success?

Neither. It's a play about the gates of horn and the gates of death and what good behaviour has to do with the gap between. A sort of parallel is the soliloquy before his death in *Richard II*. As I said, the actors were happy with the verse and it staged all right.

Sephe deals in women's lib, the synthetic quality of much modern life – and nuclear disaster. The new comedy is a treatment of terrorism and the gutter press. *The Dark Voyage* is set in the Viking period. This 'usual subject matter' of my work – as some critics emphasize it – is only a bit of the story.

In a conversation, Sir Peter Hall said he thought the verse play tradition today is being perpetuated by Beckett and Harold Pinter.

I said similar things in the *Agenda* Verse Drama issue (18.4-19.1, 1981) But quite a bit of their 'poetry', I think, has not worn too well since. It had a big period impact, but it seems to be diminishing.

A provocative comment from Glyn Pursglove in Contemporary Poets: *'Dale's finest work is that in which memory attempts to recall to language the moment of experience, to put wordless epiphany into words; the "moments" of epiphany are those in which a kind of "double exposure" makes available to the seeing mind the past or the future in the present, in memory or imagination, so that the "moment" itself becomes timeless, an awareness of mutability co-existing with an apprehension of something outside time.' Can you say something about the worldview that might cause you to see such a 'double exposure' as part of the present moment?*

I'm pleased with the comment obviously. It sums up very well what I hope some of my poems are aiming to achieve, but how to comment on it or my worldview is a problem. I'm pretty much a materialist. I hope he's using 'epiphany' in its modern critical rather than old religious sense. If it is a detailed version of Larkin's idea of wanting in a poem to preserve a moment or event so that it persists through time, he's right. The only double exposure in some of the poems lies in that they may contain a vivid momentary event but at the same time imply that it's only one of the countless many whose gestures, not personnel, persist.

Let's talk about how a particular poem came about, the circumstances that gave it life, the process of writing it, how long it took, what you revised, and so forth. Two very different poems come to mind from Under the Breath: *'Coastwise', for your son Piers, and the elliptical, rather mysterious 'Sotto Voce', from* Da Capo, *with its haunting line, 'Love is the labour we shall not complete.'*

I've always been fascinated with the difficulty of catching the lights and liveliness of water in words. There are many shots at doing different effects in the poems. 'Coastwise', then, began with the dog's-paw waves and fermented from there. From childhood on I've been sorry for all the creatures without hands. It must make life very difficult. Would we have been so brainy without fingers and thumbs? (Valéry speaks of the importance to our evolution of the opposable thumb, and adds succinctly: and the opposable soul.) It's written in the *In Memoriam* stanza and took years to clarify, written almost backwards to reach the opening line which had been floating around my head since the mid-Sixties.

Apparently there's an ancient Irish tradition which says that it is on the brink of water that poetry is revealed to the poet.

But otherwise, it describes a real situation on a real beach? You see, I've learned my lesson, I'm not taking the autobiography for granted.

A remark of Edward Thomas's in his *Maurice Maeterlinck* may make my point better: 'Whatever be the subject, the poem must not depend upon anything outside itself except the humanity of the reader ... if it does not create about itself a world of its own it is condemned to endure the death which is its element.' So I hope the poem encapsulates experience that many adults have in relation to their offspring and vice-versa.

And 'Sotto Voce'?

I suppose the source of 'Sotto Voce' is my childhood immersion in the Authorized Version, and my soaking in Yeats during the sixth-form. If I'm not misremembering – I don't keep working papers – it came almost by dictation from somewhere. I just had to take it down. I remember one line was changed much later; otherwise it was written in one session. Roethke's 'I learn by going where I have to go', first encountered in my student days, may also lurk somewhere at the back of it.

'Almost by dictation'? How do you experience that – how does it happen? Are we back to the 'female voice' you mentioned at the beginning? Or to Villon nagging you in the night?

No. This was daytime, pre-breakfast, as I recall, and the words were those of the inner voice you think in, but I wasn't thinking it. Like spoken sentences, you start without knowing the end till you get it written down. Frost speaks of never knowing the end in writing a poem until he gets to it.

You must know Czeslaw Milosz's poem on the same subject, 'Secretaries':

> I am no more than a secretary of the invisible thing
> That is dictated to me and a few others.
> Secretaries, mutually unknown, we walk the earth
> Without much comprehension. Beginning a phrase in the middle
> Or ending it with a comma. And how it all looks when completed
> Is not up to us to inquire, we won't read it anyway.

The same, or a similar, thought?

That's frequently the case, except that the poet is the first reader and also the first re-reader.

Which line was changed much later, by the way?

Line three had a rhythmic improvement made to it: 'Years out, old local maps, like the Holy Book...'

It's a haunting, epigrammatic poem — very like Roethke's 'Waking' in that sense.

If it's haunting, I'm glad. That's the quality the sequence needed.

Yet Roethke's poem is a villanelle. This one is in couplets, using pararhyme. Perhaps one shouldn't question dictation, but is it fair to ask why you decided to do it that way?

Pararhyme is more haunting than straight rhyme. Villanelles tend to be cyclical, enclosed forms; couplets in some ways are one damn thing after another, like years. So the couplet is used as a stanza to show the groping forward of the speech to an unfinished 'end'.

    I've seldom written couplets in straight rhymes: they always sound noisy to me. Someone described Pope's couplets as an ill-natured clock striking thirty-three thousand.

You said earlier that you had 'no idea' when Da Capo *would 'surface and gel. If you can't hear and get the rhythm right for the poem nothing else will work.' So how did this sequence surface and gel?*

Forster speaks like this of the creative process: 'And when the process is over, when the picture or symphony or lyric or novel (or whatever it is) is complete, the artist, looking back on it, will wonder how on earth he did it.' He compares the mystery of it all to lowering a bucket into the subconscious, fetching it up and mixing it with normal experience. While close to what happens, that sounds too deliberate. The bucket decides when to go down and when to come up and tips the stuff into normal experience and mixes it up. It's not always what the artist wants brought up.

    When I was giving up full-time work, I felt a biggish poem was pending – like a retirement clock, or that bucket. The poem now first in the sequence was done and I didn't think much more about it; it seemed finished with. Then, months later, *Sotto Voce* turned up, and collected a poem, either side, after which the thing spread either way. 'Misencounter' arrived some months after that. The 'Epitaph' in upper-case was a last-minute addition. It gave me more trouble than other parts because it had to be written almost badly: churchyard epitaphs are often a bit amateurishly put. Philip Hoy, who wrote an essay on the sequence, raised two or three queries that showed one or two phrases in the final draft of the sequence needed adjusting for clarity. I think some punctuation changes were made to the limited edition version for the *Under the Breath* text.

The mysterious 'Lena Latimer (1939-1992)' is a poem that looks almost like a dedication, in form and layout on the page. Is she the inspiration for these poems? Who was she?

She's a dramatic character. (One of my mother's names was in fact Lena but the name was needed for the euphony with Latimer, so that oddity is a red-herring.) She represents any one of those lovers that all of us of either sex may have had when young. Old crocks look back and wonder how different life might have been with one of those partners, the risks and opportunities taken or not, so many years ago: 'the road not taken'; 'the awful daring of a moment's surrender', or not!

Everyone wants to know about how poets work. So when do you write? How do you write? Do you write every day? How long does it usually take you to finish a poem? I believe you've said that it sometimes takes years.

It can vary between poems written straight down and those that have tricky passages that may take months or years to clarify, for the lid to click shut. I get up early and write and polish best usually then, often before or during breakfast. Pauline breakfasts later. In the last two decades or so, some poems arrive almost ready-made and it's a quick nip into the study to scrawl them down. The process is unpredictable: a complete villanelle turned up when I was in the middle of revising a bit of Laforgue – translations are worked on later in the day. One poem, 'Parting Gift', came into my head in the middle of an opera we were attending, which was most inconvenient of it. After finishing *One Another*, with one sonnet I waited over thirteen years for the last line to settle; another took eighteen months for the sestet to clarify.

For polishing and correction I prefer to work with fountain-pen or micro-ball on large sheets. My handwriting's minute. I prefer black ink on big sheets so that the surrounding white space concentrates the mind. Once I've an inkling of a poem, all other work is shelved because it takes the mind over until a viable draft is clear. Once the draft gets somewhere, it's moved to word-processor and I can relax. I keep annual pocket books for finished poems, leaving the recto blank for any late tunings or developments.

I'd like to ask you about a comment of yours, made in the early Seventies, about the short poem: 'Finally, a writer risks everything in this form. Success is awesome; but failure is total, a word or rhythm wrong, a falsity of tone or image, and nothing is left.' That sounds awfully apocalyptic. Has age softened this judgment?

That was in a review of Michael Fried's *The Powers*, from 1972. My view hasn't changed much. Picasso spoke of when one more stroke applied to a painting left the thing ruined. Yeats remarked on the moment when the last element goes in and 'a poem comes right with a click like a closing box'. It may be harder to hear the lid shut when writing free verse. Nearly all polishing off, in my experience, is a question of curtailment.

In your interview with Ian Hamilton, you lamented, 'I have written too much.' Do you really think so? You've got eight or nine collections of poetry, half-a-dozen volumes of translations, and of course your criticism.

Perhaps too much, particularly prose. I was trying to cheer him up. Because of all the journalism he had to do, Ian infrequently had time to turn his hand to poetry. It's the opposite tendency with nearly all artists: to create too much. Yet, if you're aiming at an ideal, the perfect poem, while there's life you keep trying. You don't have much option.

Later, Ian wrote in my copy of a small selection of the prolific Swinburne he'd edited: 'It's not my fault.'

What did he mean by that?

He'd have cut more, but it had to be commercial book length. Most poets write too much. It's an occupational hazard. On the other hand, if you write too little, scholars are tempted to scrabble about for uncollected poems, near-finishes, and drafts to make the oeuvre book-length and scholar-worth. Larkin, once asked whether a new book was in the offing, remarked that he had enough poems for a volume but not enough stuff to space them out with. He published sparingly even so, but there's a lot of stuff in that *Collected* of his, edited by Anthony Thwaite.

At least in America, poets are encouraged to publish a lot, and perhaps use their wastebaskets too rarely – often, to meet the pressures of publishers or tenure committees, one suspects. What is your opinion of the current wastebasket-to-publisher ratio?

Far too much is published on both sides of the Atlantic. Yet some poets have to write a lot to produce a small number of fine poems and perhaps don't discard all they might. Others, like Housman or Eliot, produce a small amount to a fairly standard high level. Even so, Housman is repetitious. Discarding poems can be a hesitant business. As you get older, you're frequently surprised by what poems of yours critics and readers prefer, what gets taken for anthologies. So some poets hesitate to junk any effusion; others try to write less verse to focus other people's range of choice on their best poems.

You've written two interesting poems about two interesting poets: Robinson Jeffers and Yvor Winters, both men you never met. Jeffers has attracted a very disparate following – from Dana Gioia to Czeslaw Milosz. What attracted you to this odd, gigantic figure in American literature?

I was puzzled by his rhythms and spent a long time trying to unravel how he achieved them in his best shorter poems, some very powerful. He was also his own man, whatever the literary world might think. And he risked his hand at plays, of course.

Winters's criticism interested me, particularly on Valéry and Hopkins, and one or two of his poems stick in my mind. His discussion, in 'The Audible Reading of Poetry', of the rarity and difficulty of true spondees, was also intriguing.

Incidentally, I once upset some Wintersians at a summer school in London by suggesting good metrical uses for what I'd call even spondees, iambic spondees and trochaic spondees, recognizing three forms.

Why did that upset them?

I'm not really sure. I was a bit surprised. Winters seems to have made them think that the true spondee was a difficult thing to achieve in English verse. It isn't – though the other types may be more common. The students seemed upset that an Englishman should disagree with their guru. I was puzzled by the strength of his influence on them. It seemed almost domination.

I've been to the room you describe – the room Jeffers died in. It's an amazing room, and an amazing house, built by Jeffers himself using the local granite, cosy and austere at once. And yes, as you say,

> *clear with dawnlight or the storm light,*
> *noise of the great sea crashing beyond.*

You write that:

> *You whose words live on*
> *have given me, unlike the Christ,*
> *a place to die.*

A cardinal sin to ask, I know, but could you elaborate on those lines a little?

When I worked in hospital in my student days, a doctor remarked that he often found some Christians the worst and noisiest at dying because they worried about which place came next, whereas agnostics just accepted the end as the end. You get that acceptance in Jeffers.
    I have a colour photo of the room and the tower but I've never been there. That poem was written for *The Tribute of his Peers: Elegies for Robinson Jeffers*, edited by Robert Zaller and published by Tor House Press.

Like Jeffers, Winters was an uncompromising, rigorous, idiosyncratic figure. I suppose it's a tendency in West Coast writers. Could you explain how the Winters poem came about?

Reading his work again, I rediscovered in *Maule's Curse* a kind of darkness that it seemed the rationalizing of his criticism was trying to contain in the best way he could. This dichotomy became interesting and the poem drew a connection with 'nuclear dread' – the fact that rationally derived nuclear electricity gave light but also deadly danger. There had been accidents at nuclear plants, such as Windscale. I think Three Mile Island may have been later.

Yes, you conclude:

> I shape these words, the almost foreign parlance
> we both imagine ours as born and bred,
> and weave your myth of reason against all jargons,
> here in this study lit by nuclear dread.

There was so much Age of Aquarius mumbo-jumbo about that it seemed not a bad idea to suggest that reason, despite where it had got us then, was a myth more worthwhile to cherish than most of that.

It is a myth: I remember McNamara arguing that if Moscow set up a defensive missile system round the city it would be an aggressive act because the balance of power would be upset if America could not deliver instant retaliatory annihilation – or, of course, surprise attacks, which he never mentioned. It was another myth that any systems could render nuclear power stations safe from human fallibility.

Still, we needed to stick with reason, though not with nuclear power. There wasn't much else that worked as well as had the myth that we are reasonable beings. Perhaps, as Winters thought, even in poetry we should stick by reason.

Winters is understandable and straightforward. I don't agree with him much, but I can see how he got where he did. Try reasoning through some of Leavis's positions. Winters may have been frequently wrong or obtuse; nevertheless he's an interesting critic to learn things from, even by disagreement.

How much do you really think a common language divides us?

To be facetious, you've increased my doubts about it with your remarks on the 'ah' assonance in 'Half Light'. It unites more than it divides us, but it may occasionally mislead us either side of the ocean. That line you quote was meant to glance at Shaw's remark about two nations divided by the same language. I was mindful, too, of Wyatt Prunty's piece.

The one he wrote about you and another West Coast poet, Timothy Steele? 'Though there are differences ... these two poets generally sound alike. And this is because they are writing formal poetry derived from a tradition which persists on both sides of the Atlantic.' By the way, Steele himself was part of Winters's extended circle of influence at Stanford. I don't follow the logic of why Winters must be speaking a similar language.

In the last verse of the poem, the shared 'almost foreign parlance' refers metaphorically to the language of reason – which the poem suggests that Winters and the speaker shared. I didn't quite agree with Wyatt's close analysis of my English rhythms. The differences in the two versions of English can be subtle and are growing; verbs and tenses differ; the uses of auxiliary verbs differ; most of all, pronunciation and stressing differ. These things impinge more on verse, perhaps, than conversation or prose. It was a shock when I first heard Frost and Marianne Moore read their work; poems from teenage imagined in my own head with different sounds, pace, pitch and sometimes rhythms. So yes, we speak similar languages but we have to work warily to make sure we understand the nuances properly. Bush's use of the word 'crusade' for the war on terrorism sounds like a gaffe this side of the ocean but I'm told it was deliberate.

Take Frost, for example. 'The Oven-Bird' – of which there are two species, neither of them seen here – has a straight-forward top meaning, but I've read somewhere that its call is given in America as: 'teacher-teacher'. It would be just like the old fox to have added that extra level. His views on teachers are well known. It works well until the last line, perhaps. If any of this is there, many British readers might miss it, not knowing the bird or its call.

You are fond, I believe, of this passage from Sir Philip Sidney:

> *'But if...you cannot bear the planet-like music of poetry; if you have so earth-creeping a mind that it cannot lift itself up to look to the sky of poetry...[a] curse I must send you in the behalf of all poets: that while you live, you live in love, and never get favour for lacking skill of a sonnet; and when you die, your memory die from the earth, for want of an epitaph.'*

It's a nice and gentle sort of curse.

Obviously, this comes from a culture where poetry occupies a much more central place than it does in ours. What would it take for poetry to be more integrated into our society than it is today? What would it take for it to reach a broader audience of readers?

I don't know. Not poetry slams, I think, and not more prizes and competitions. Better poets, perhaps? Fewer impostors? Less media hype of all and everything; less information overload? But since Pope's Homer, Byron's romantic tales and Tennyson's *In Memoriam*, poets have wishfully expected their audiences to be large. Before that time, for lyric poetry they probably never were: hand-written copies were all that could be hoped for, distributed among the poet's friends and acquaintances. Maybe the whole problem was encapsulated by Donne's publisher of 1633, opening his 'The Printer to the Understanders' with these remarks: 'For this time I must speak only to you: at another, *Readers* may perchance serve my turne; and I thinke this a way very free from exception, in hope that very few will have a minde to confesse themselves ignorant.' In other words, new books of verse will have fewer understanders than 'readers' and, as with the response to much modernist work, people will profess to understand their reading rather than risk appearing foolish. So perhaps, along with Donne and Milton, contemporary poets must put up with fit audience though few, and even fewer 'understanders' than it may appear.

Auden tries to make the best of the situation in the opening of 'In the Cave of Making'. Betjeman and Dylan Thomas and others managed to get some media fame, but how far were they subverted or diverted, and how much of their work will last? Come to that, will anything? We live in a disposable culture, after all. Perhaps a few gentle curses like Sidney's might be permitted?

Can we conclude on a more humorous note with a poem – this one not by you, but about you?

Yes, if you like.

You noted earlier that cycling helped you escape the isolation and loneliness of your childhood years. You stayed a cyclist, as the following poem by Humphrey Clucas notes:

HEAD CASE

*The day you fell on your head,
Your cycle-club, unnerved by so much blood,
Took you for dead.*

*And how should we have grieved?
Your sort of honesty's not widely loved.
Your own, bereaved;*

> *Certain friends distressed.*
> *'Poor chap – another poet bites the dust.*
> *We've had his best,*
>
> *I imagine.' (Who can tell?)*
> *Sheepishly, you own to a thick skull.*
> *Dear friend, it serves you well.*

Well, it's better than Dryden's

> The midwife placed her hand on thy thick skull
> With this prophetic blessing, 'Be thou dull!'

Perhaps unwisely, I'd mentioned to Humphrey that the x-ray operator had said mine was the thickest skull he had ever dealt with. Presumably that's why it hadn't fractured. I have given bikes up now.

□

And There Was Light

i. m. R. D.

Sun through the autumn pear-trees,
leaves a translucent flock of ambers
like benign fire.

The beauty is not in the air,
not in the leaves, not in the lambency
but in the mind's eye

that is dying – stark staring.
Not enough, the spectral ambience.
What was it, light?

Eyes that have seen you fare
lampless into the curtained blackout.
Brother, our long good bye.

Lead

The soldiers have long been broken or lost,
the mends a slight relief when missed,
the matchstick-mounted heads, plasticine arms.
– And that trilbied farmer,
feet bent off by his tractor,
who got the knack of stilts.
All of them mourned in their time.

Yet in the lost child's eye
that glisten of the hidden lead
the inner gleam of a loved thing
never again so lighted on.

ORIEL

The seasons are all wrong these days.
Silhouetted in the unweeping willow
a few late migrant birds,
semiquavers.
The last dead leaves on sharper view.

A ghost flits in the oriel opposite,
into light, then back from the window.
The silver birch, gust swayed,
puppet masters
the to and fro-ing wraith of the sill.

Half turned you muse over the gardens
part of a picture not where you are.
Skies, sheaves – burrs in your hair?
Past laughter
a sycamore seed-wing at the corner of your eye.

SOLILOQUY

I used to say:
'You go to sleep now,'
and you would.

You knew it would take
hours for me,
to catch you up.

And I'm still here,
you poor old thing,
still awake,

talking in your sleep,
trying not to say,
not to wake you:

'Sleep, my dearest,
stay asleep.'
– Whispers as if

tomorrow we'll both
be here
in our old love.

With Robert Gray, 1956

Abinger, 1957

Isle of Wight, 1957

Prefects' Room, Strode's School, 1958

Pauline Strouvelle, 1958

Sheringham, late 1950s

With Pauline, on their honeymoon, 1963

Pauline, with Piers (left) and Kim, 1968

1968

The Storms, 1968    *Mortal Fire*, 1970

François Villon: Selected Poems, 1978

Bournemouth, 1982

AGENDA

PETER DALE
FIFTIETH BIRTHDAY ISSUE

Agenda, 26:2, Summer 1988

EARTH LIGHT

Peter Dale

HIPPOPOTAMUS PRESS

Earth Light, 1991

Portrait of Peter Dale, by Eddie Wolfram, 1992, © Peter Dale

In Eddie Wolfram's Studio, London Fields, 1996

Edge to Edge, 1996    Dante, *The Divine Comedy*, 1996

1998, courtesy of Erminia Passannanti ©

1998, courtesy of Erminia Passannanti ©

Poems of Jules Laforgue, 2001

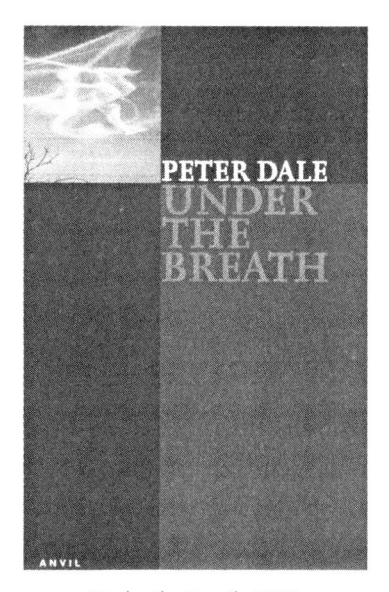

Under the Breath, 2002

Bibliography

While everything has been done to ensure the completeness and accuracy of this bibliography, the compilers can be sure their efforts have not been entirely successful. The editors would therefore be pleased to hear from anyone who can identify omissions or errors, which it would be their hope to repair in future editions.

Primary Works

Books of Poems

Nerve (Privately printed, Addlestone, Surrey, 1959) [200 signed copies, stapled, hand numbered, no page numbers; copies vary as central pages were removed from some].

Walk from the House (Fantasy Press, Oxford, 1962).

The Storms (Macmillan, London, 1968).

Mortal Fire (Macmillan, London, 1970).

Mortal Fire: Selected Poems (Agenda Editions, London, 1976 / Ohio University Press, Athens, 1976) [Adds over fifty poems and the verse play "The Cell" to the original 1970 collection].

Cross-Channel (Hippopotamus Press, Sutton, Surrey, 1977) [Poems and verse-translations].

One Another: A Sonnet Sequence (Carcanet New Press, Manchester/Agenda Editions, London, 1978).

Too Much of Water: Poems 1976-82 (Agenda Editions, London, 1983).

A Set of Darts: Epigrams for the Nineties [with W. S. Milne and Robert Richardson] (Big Little Poem Books, Grimsby, South Humberside, 1990).

Earth Light (Hippopotamus Press, Frome, Somerset, 1991) [Issued in both hardback and paperback].

Edge to Edge: New and Selected Poems (Anvil Press, London, 1996).

Under the Breath (Anvil Press, London, 2002).

One Another (The Waywiser Press, London, 2002) [Revised, second edition].

Limited and Fine Editions of Poems

Mortal Fire (Academy Editions, London, 1970) [Limited edition of 100 signed copies].

Cross-Channel (Hippopotamus Press, Sutton, Surrey, 1977) [Poems and verse-translations; 25 copies signed].

Too Much of Water: Poems 1976-82 (Agenda Editions, London, 1983) [Limited edition of 200 signed copies].

'Sparrow', *The Big Little Poem Series*, No. 11, edited by Robert Richardson (High Wycombe, Bucks, 1983).

'Thanks', 'Gifts', 'Spring', *The Big Little Poem Series*, No. 12, edited by Robert Richardson (Grimsby, October 1985).

Earth Light (Hippopotamus Press, Frome, Somerset, 1991) [Limited to 10 copies in hardback signed by PD].

'Steps', *Six Twentieth Century Poets*, edited by Anthony Selbourne and etched and printed by John T. Freeman (Bull Head Press, The Peter Goodall Gallery, Guildford, 1990 / Making Waves, Guildford, 1991) [Limited edition of 100; Calligraphic text by Peneli].

Da Capo: A Sequence (Poets and Painters Press, Agenda Editions, London, 1997) [Limited to 200 copies, 50 signed by author; Introductory essay by Philip Hoy].

'Wishful', 'Coastwise', and 'Home Ground', *Kids' Stuff, Door-to-Everywhere Series*, No. 10, edited by Robert Richardson (Melton Mowbray, Leicestershire, 2000) [Broadside].

'An Old Song', 'Skirt', and 'Wish', *Hindsight, Door-to-Everywhere Series*, No. 23, edited by Robert

Richardson (Melton Mowbray, Leicestershire, 2002) [Broadside].

Ephemera and Private Publications

'Things thought too long can be no longer thought ...' (Drian Galleries, London, April 1971) [Introduction in catalogue of exhibition of Eddie Wolfram's paintings].
'Dying', Press release for *A Set of Darts: Epigrams for the Nineties* [with W. S. Milne and Robert Richardson] (Big Little Poem Books, Grimsby, South Humberside, 1990) [Epigram].
'A Time to Speak', *Some Poems from Anvil Press* (Anvil Press Poetry, London, 2000) [Publicity pamphlet].
'Half Light', Programme of Rainbow Poetry Group for a reading held on 11 October 2000, Hove.
'The Walk', *Anvil Press Poetry Ltd Catalogue*, 2003.
'Mary's Carol', *The Rainbow Poetry News* (Brighton), 7, July 2004: 9.

Books of Verse Translations

The Legacy, The Testament, and Other Poems of François Villon (Macmillan, London, 1973 / St. Martin's Press, New York, 1973).
The Seasons of Cankam: Love Poems Translated from the Tamil [with Kokilam Subbiah] (Agenda Editions, London, 1975).
Selected Poems of François Villon (Penguin Books, Harmondsworth, 1978, 1988, 1994) [Bilingual, with introduction and notes; Some revisions in each impression].
Narrow Straits: Poems from the French (Hippopotamus Press, Frome, Somerset, 1985) [Bilingual, with introduction].
Poems of Jules Laforgue (Anvil Press Poetry, London, 1986) [Bilingual, with introduction and notes; Reprinted with additional poems, 2001].
The Divine Comedy (Anvil Press Poetry, London, 1996, 1998, 2001, 2003, 2004) [Terza-rima version, with introduction; Each printing with revisions].
Poems of François Villon: The Legacy, The Testament & Other Poems (Anvil Press Poetry, London, 2001) [Bilingual translation with introduction and notes by PD; Contains additional poems not included in the earlier Penguin edition].
Corbière, Tristan, *Wry-Blue Loves and Other Poems/Les Amours jaunes* (Anvil Press Poetry, London, 2005) [Bilingual text, with introduction and notes].

Limited and Fine Editions of Translations

The Legacy and Other Poems of François Villon (Agenda Editions, London, 1971) [400 copies, 100 on hand-made paper, signed by PD].
Villon (Macmillan, London, 1973 / St Martins Press, New York, 1973) [Quarter-leather, marbled endpapers and illustrated with woodcuts by Michael Denning].
The Seasons of Cankam, with Kokilam Subbiah (Agenda Editions, London, 1975) [Signed].
Narrow Straits (Hippopotamus Press, Frome, Somerset, 1985) [Bilingual, French poets, with introduction; Limited to 10 copies numbered and signed].
The Divine Comedy (Anvil Press Poetry, 1996) [Terza-rima version; edition of two copies, bound in red goatskin, marbled endpapers].
At an Odd Angle, Door-to-Everywhere Series, No. 15, edited by Robert Richardson (Melton Mowbray, Leicestershire, 2001) [Broadsheet, translations by PD of three poems by Erminia Passannanti: 'Dialogue between Two Chairs', 'The King, the Words', 'W la Revoluçion'].

Plays

The Cell, *Agenda*, 13:2, Summer 1975 [Also published in *Mortal Fire* (Agenda Editions, London, 1976 / Ohio University Press, Athens, 1976)].

Sephe, Agenda, 18:4-19:1, Spring 1981: 8-76 [Verse Drama Double Issue].
The Dark Voyage, Agenda, 29:1-2, Spring-Summer 1991: 45-77.

CRITICISM

An Introduction to Rhyme (Bellew/Agenda Editions, London, 1998).

INTERVIEWS

'Jon Silkin Interview', *Agenda*, 4:1, April-May 1965: 41-48.
'Peter Dale interviewed by the Editor of *Outposts*', *Outposts*, 156, Spring 1988: 50-57.
'Grilled Poet – Peter Dale', *Schools Poetry Review*, 18, April 1989: 15-16 [Interviewed by James Sale].
'Ian Hamilton in Conversation with Peter Dale', *Agenda*, 31:2, Summer 1993: 7-21 [The Sixties Issue].
Görtschacher, Wolfgang, 'Interview with Peter Dale (Agenda)', *Little Magazine Profiles: The Little Magazines in Great Britain, 1939-1993* (University of Salzburg, Salzburg, 1993): 330-344.
Michael Hamburger in Conversation with Peter Dale (Between the Lines, London, 1998).
Anthony Thwaite in Conversation with Peter Dale and Ian Hamilton (Between the Lines, London, 1999).
Richard Wilbur in Conversation with Peter Dale (Between the Lines, London, 2000).
Vianu, Lidia, 'Interview with Peter Dale', *Desperado Literature* (2001): < http://www.lidiavianu.go.ro/peter_dale.htm >.

INTRODUCTIONS TO BOOKS BY OTHER AUTHORS

'Mugging or Translation', *Anthracite*, selected poems of Bartoli Cattafi, translated by Brian Cole (Arc Publications, Todmorden, 2000): 15-19 [Visible Poets Series].

TRANSLATIONS OF PETER DALE'S POEMS BY OTHERS

How Very Different the Tastes: A Selection of British Poetry, 1970-81, edited by Ben Bal (Stichting Workshop Amsterdam School Press, Amsterdam, 1982): 12 [Translation of 'Sleep', with notes].
Daems, Catherine and Franz de Haes, *Miroirs, Fenêtres Le Courrier*, 182, April-June 1989: 5-25 [Translation of 'Mirrors, Windows', a sonnet sequence in *Earth Light*].
Daems, Catherine and Franz de Haes, *Le Journal des Poètes* (Brussels), 8, December 1993: 10 [Translation of 'A Time to Speak' and 'Answer'].
Passannanti, Erminia, 'Gesto', 'Tacito', 'Il Sentiero infossato', *Immaginazione* (Italy) January-February 1998: 4-6 [Translation of 'Gesture', 'Unspoken', and 'The Sunken Path', with an introduction].

UNCOLLECTED POEMS

'Duologue', *Painter and Sculptor*, 1958, and *Gemini* (Oxford), Spring 1960.
'Pirates', 'When I was bored', *Oxford Opinion*, 5 March 1960.
'Thomas', 'Mary', 'Reed', *Breakthrough* (Oxford), October 1960.
'The Passing of an Old Lady', *Tomorrow*, 4, 1960: 12; *Universities' Poetry*, 4, edited by Richard Tillinghast and Clive Jordan, Keele, April 1962: 35.
'Hawk the Wren', 'The Faces (St Peter's Hospital)', *Oxford Opinion* (Oxford), Michaelmas 1960 [Early version of 'Meditation down the Wards'].
'Nearly Got the Moon in', *Oxford Opinion* (Hilary), 1961.
'No One of Importance', *Granta-Oxford Opinion* (Hilary), 1961: 49.
'Not this Wine', *Oxford Opinion* (Oxford), 1961.[?]
'The Blade', broadcast on BBC Third Programme, 17 July 1961.
'Gentlemas for my Mother', *Isis* (Trinity), 1961.

'Once upon a day, xi.58', 'Beggar selling Matches, iv.59', 'Novel in brief, i.60', *Isis* (Trinity), 8 November 1961: 11.
'Nearly Got the Moon In', *Agenda*, 2.6, February-March 1962: 7-9.
'Walk from the house', *Universities' Poetry*, 4, edited by Richard Tillinghast and Clive Jordan, April 1962: 36 [Version differs from that of *Edge to Edge*].
'Letter Which I Did Not Post', *Stand*, 6.3, Autumn 1963 [Early version].
'Overnight Coach', *Universities' Poetry*, 5, edited by Tom Lowenstein and Ken Smith, May 1963: 36 [Version differs from that of *Edge to Edge*].
'Transatlantic', *Agenda*, 3:3, December 1963-January 1964: 4.
'Whither thou goest', *The Listener*, 29 December 1966.
'Elegy', *Tribune*, 12 January 1968.
'Still Life', *Shenandoah*, 20:4, Summer 1969.
'Façade', *New York Times*, 14 October 1969.
'In Memory of a Hungarian Poet Murdered by the Nazis', *The Young British Poets*, edited by Jeremy Robson (Chatto and Windus, London, 1971): 39.
'Night', *Tribune*, 18 February 1972.
'Unposted Letter', *Poetry of the Committed Individual*, edited by Jon Silkin (Gollancz, London, 1973): 109 [See also under 'Student Work' for earlier version].
'Orpheus to Eurydice', *Agenda*, 16:3-4, Autumn-Winter 1978-79: 74.
'Eurydice to Orpheus', *Agenda*, 16:3-4, Autumn-Winter 1978-79: 75.
'Lullaby', *Poetry Review*, 68:4, January 1979: 28.
'Feud', *Agenda*, 19:2-3, Summer 1982: 14.
'Stroll', *Thames Poetry*, 2:13, October 1983: 38.
'Reproach', *Proof*, 5:3, January 1984: 2.
'Recreation Ground', *Poetry Book Society Anthology*, edited by Jonathan Barker (December 1986): 26 [Early draft version].
'Song', *Outposts*, 161, Summer 1989: 32.
'Aubade', *Exile*, 14:2, Toronto, 1989: 66.
'It's Time', 'Words', *Outposts*, 167, Winter 1990: 31.
'Broken Sleep', 'Right of Reply', *The Swansea Review*, 8, October 1991: 9, 11.
'Haunts (For E.T.)', *Acumen*, 16, October 1992: 32 [Misprinted, remove 'un-'].
'Hoar Frost and Rime', *Physic Meet and Metaphysic: A Celebration on Edward Lowbury's 80th Birthday*, edited by Yann Lovelock (University of Salzburg Press, Salzburg, 1993): 79.
'Valerian', *Acumen*, 20, October 1994: 61.
'The Keepsake', 'Old Song', *Agenda*, 31:4-32:2, Spring 1994: 238, 240.
'An Old Man Considers the Snow', *New Poetry Quarterly*, 1, September 1994: 94.
'Way Out: For E. W.', *Agenda*, 32:3-4, Autumn-Winter 1994-95: 147 [A Tribute to Peter Russell: Special Issue].
'Redress', 'The Dead (1939-45)', *Stand*, 37:4, Autumn 1996: 7.
'Reconciliation', *Outposts*, 183, 1997: 18.
'Dying Words (An Old Woman Speaks)', *Stand*, 39:4, Autumn 1998: 77.
'19', *The New Exeter Book of Riddles*, edited by Kevin Crossley-Holland and Lawrence Sail (Enitharmon Press, London, 1999): unnumbered.
'Dale's Preamble', *Poems of François Villon: The Legacy, The Testament & Other Poems* (Anvil Press Poetry, London, 2001): 13 [See: 'Verse Translations' section above].
'Jigsaw', *The Interpreter's House*, 19, February 2002: 15.
'Tidying Up', *The Rialto*, 52, Winter 2002-03: 38 [Erroneously listed as p. 12 on contents page].
'Peace', *Acumen*, 46, May 2003: 9.
'Second Reading', *London Magazine*, June-July 2003: 29.
'Christening', 'Birthday List', *Stand*, 5:2, September 2003: 38-39.
'Night-piece', *Acumen*, 47, September 2003: 74.
'Second Reading', 'Orpheus in Darkness', 'The Last Nursery Rhyme', 'Cameo', *Agenda*, 39:4, Summer 2003: 214, 321, 322, 323 [Celebratory issue for William Cookson].
'Villanelle', 'Over the Other Side', *The Swansea Review*, 22, 2003: 119-120 [Versions earlier than collected texts].
'Villanelle', 'Footbridge', *Dream Catcher*, 2004 [Revised version].
'Playtime', 'Rearguard', *Acumen*, 50, 2004: 77.

UNCOLLECTED EPIGRAMS

'Walk', *Agenda*, 9:4-10:1, Winter 1971-72: 91.
'Dream', *The Review*, 29-30, Spring-Summer 1972: 85.
'Salute', *Outposts*, Autumn 1983: 17 [40th Anniversary Issue; Co-signed by William Cookson, but written by PD].
'Flotsam', *Agenda*, 21:4-22:1, Winter 1983-Spring 1984: 20.
'Echo', epigraph to sheet music of *Echo and Narcissus*, a piece for solo flute by Nigel Clarke, 6 September 1984.
'Eliot', *Agenda*, 23:1-2, Summer 1985: 182 [T.S. Eliot Special Issue].
'Preface', *Acumen*, 10, October 1989: 69.
'Literacy', 'Hardy: Aged Eighty-Eight', 'Slim Volume', 'Bard', 'Genius', *The Use of English*, 42:2, Spring 1991: 14, 19.
'Parents' Evening', 'Poetic Immortality', *Acumen*, 14, October 1991: 62.
'Peace', 'Haunts', 'Thesaurus', 'Gloom', 'Exorcising the Dog', 'Friendship', *The Swansea Review*, 8, October 1991: 7-9.
'Thanks', *Homage to Imagism*, edited by William Pratt and Robert Richardson (AMS Press, London & New York, 1992): 51.
'Time Travel', *The Swansea Review*, 13, November 1994: 91.
'With the Gift of a Book', *The Formalist*, 5:2, 1994: 80.
'Cat and That', 'Cascade', *The Churchill Clarion* (Woking), July 1994 [Early version of 'Cat and That'].
'Birthday Wishes: For Mairi MacInnes', 'Poetry Library', 'Poetry Library II', *A Tribute to Mairi MacInnes*, edited by Peter Robinson (Shoestring Press, Nottingham, 2005): 42.

UNCOLLECTED TRANSLATIONS

Apollinaire, 'Rhenish Night', *Modern Poets of Europe: A Selection*, edited by Patricia and William Oxley (Spiny Babbler, Nepal, 2003): 85.
Aragon, Louis, 'The Lilacs and the Roses', *Outposts*, 180-181, 1995: 104.
Baudelaire, Charles, 'The Albatross', *Acumen*, 16, October 1992: 75.
– 'Man and the Sea', *Acumen*, 6, October 1987: 75.
– 'The Voyage', *Exile* (Toronto), 14:2, 1989: 68-74 [Misprinted].
– 'The Jewels' in 'Nude Studies in French Verse', *In Other Words* (Journal of the Translators' Association), 7, Summer 1996: 24-28.
– 'Undulant and Opalescent the Robes', *Baudelaire in English*, edited by Carol Clark and Robert Sykes (Penguin, London, 1997): 43 [Revised from *Narrow Straits*].
Brines, Francisco, 'Evening Temptations', *Agenda*, 35:2, Summer 1997: 58 [From prose drafts and notes by Jordi Doce; Spanish Issue].
Cankam, 'Five Versions from the Classical Tamil', *Outposts*, 154, Autumn 1987: 72-75.
– 'Versions of Three Poems from Cankam', *Agenda*, 35:4-36:1, Spring 1998: 190-193 [With a note; Updated versions of poems from the book *The Seasons of Cankam*].
Corbière Tristan, 'Paper Flower', *Delta*, 55, December 1976: 15.
– 'Pariah', *The Antigonish Review*, 71-72, Autumn-Winter 1987-88: 90-93 [Reprinted in *Outposts*, 162, Autumn 1989: 14-15].
– 'Little Corpse Good for a Laugh', *Cumberland Poetry Review* (Nashville), 7:2, Spring 1988: 10-11.
– 'The Wandering Minstrel and the Pardon of St Anne', *Exile* (Toronto), 12:3, 1988: 18-26 [Reprinted in *Outposts*, 170, Autumn 1991: 16-24].
– 'Rock-a-Bye Baby', *Cumberland Poetry Review* (Nashville), 7:2, Spring 1988: 12-13.
– 'The Toad', *Core*, 2, June 1988: 4.
– 'That', *Acumen*, 11, April 1990: 74-75 [Misprinted].
– 'Tin-Whistle', *The Swansea Review*, 8, October 1991: 9.
– 'Baneflower', *The Swansea Review*, 8, October 1991: 10.
– '1 Sonnet', *The Swansea Review*, 14, October 1995: 14.
– 'Commonplace Bedtime', *The Swansea Review*, 14, October 1995: 24.
– 'Paris by Night', See under 'Exhibition Inclusions'.
Costafreda, Alfonso, 'That Disturbing Visit', *Agenda*, 35:2, Summer 1997: 23 [From prose drafts and

notes by Jordi Doce; An Anthology of Spanish Poetry].
Cros, Charles, 'Studio Scene', *Modern Painters*, 9:1, Spring 1996: 111 [See also: 'Morning' in 'Nude Studies in French Verse', *In Other Words* (Journal of the Translators' Association), 7, 1996: 24-26].
Dante: Canto 15, *Inferno*, *Agenda*, 23:1-2, Spring-Summer 1985: 92-96 [Early draft; T. S. Eliot Issue].
– "Sestina to the Woman in Green", *Agenda: An Anthology* (Carcanet, London, 1994; 1996): 237 [Revised version in *An Introduction to Rhyme* (Bellew, London, 1998): 25-26].
Follain, Jean, 'Nine Poems', *Agenda*, 15:4, Winter 1977-78: 59-63 [Includes note].
Guillevic, Eugène, 'Song', *Outposts*, 162, Autumn 1989: 16.
Laforgue, Jules, 'Complaint of Certain Tediums', *The Churchill Clarion* (Woking, Surrey), July 1995: 15 [Part, revision ms and typescript].
– 'Advertisement', concluding article 'Laforgue Revisited', *In Other Words* (Journal of the Translators' Association), 13-14, Autumn-Winter 1999-2000: 45 [Version differs from that in *Poems of Jules Laforgue*, 2001].
Mallarmé, Stéphane, versions of 'La Sainte' and 'Le Vièrge, le vivace, et le bel aujourd'hui', in an essay, 'Rime and Reason', *La Tribune Internationale des Langues Vivantes* (Perros-Guirec, France, 2001).
Meschonnic, Henri, 'Three Poems', *Agenda*, 15:4, Winter 1977-78: 65 [Published using pseudonym].
Passannanti, Erminia, 'Snail', *Agenda*, 37:1, Summer 1999: 51.
'The King, the Words', *In Other Words* (Journal of the Translators' Association), 13-14, Autumn-Winter 1999-2000: 144 [Mistitled with 'In Memoriam' running head].
'Dialogue between Two Chairs', 'The King, the Words', 'W la Revoluçion', *Door-to-Everywhere Series*, No. 15, edited by Robert Richardson (Melton Mowbray, Leicestershire, 2001).
Rimbaud, Arthur, 'First Evening' in 'Nude Studies in French Verse', *In Other Words* (Journal of the Translators' Association), 7, 1996: 24-28.
Sappho, 'Some Idea of Sappho's Ode to Anactoria', *Agenda*, 16:3-4, Autumn-Winter 1978-79: 11.
Strindberg, 'The Weathervane Sings' [with Malin Andrews], *The Swedish Book Review*, 1987: 40-41.
Tardieu, Jean, 'The Île de France', *Chronicles*, 1987: 10.
– 'Headland', *Outposts*, 162, Autumn 1989: 17.
Valéry, Paul, 'The Insinuant', 'The Woman Sleeping', *Modern Poets of Europe*, edited by Patricia and William Oxley (Spiny Babbler, Nepal, 2003): 83-84 [Revisions from *Narrow Straits*].
Verlaine, 'It Weeps in my Heart', *Agenda*, 12:4-13:1, Winter-Spring 1975: 90.
– 'Autumn Song', *Agenda*, 12:4-13:1, Winter-Spring 1975: 91.
Versions (four) from the Chinese (from notes by John Cayley), *Agenda*, 20:3-4, Autumn 1982-Winter 1983: 15-16 [Chinese Poetry Issue].

POEMS USED IN EXAMINATION PAPERS

'Eighth Period', Cambridge Institute of Education, Certificate Examination, Bedford College of Higher Education (Polhill), 16 May 1977: 2.

ACKNOWLEDGEMENTS, EPIGRAPHS, CITATIONS, QUOTATIONS

The Soul of Medicine: An Anthology of Illness and Healing, edited by Peter Adams (Arkana/Penguin, London, 1998): 76 [Last verse of 'Visitors'].
Berry, Neil, *Articles of Faith* (The Waywiser Press, London, 2002): 14 [Acknowledgements].
Campbell, James, *Thom Gunn in Conversation with James Campbell* (Between the Lines, London, 2000): 104 ['The Critics' section].
Clucas, Humphrey, 'Dedication', *Versions of Catullus* (Agenda Editions, London, 1985): 3.
Cook, Eileen, *Against Coercion: Games Poets Play* (Stanford University Press, Stanford, 1998): 302.
Cookson, William, *A Guide to the Cantos of Ezra Pound* (Anvil Press Poetry, London, 2000): xvii.
Cookson, William, 'Tom Scott', *Agenda*, 33:3-4, Autumn-Winter 1996: 314 [Obituary, Irish Issue].
Cookson, William, *Vestiges 1955-1995* (Agenda Editions/Big Little Poems Books, London, 1995): 38 [Acknowledgements].
Cookson, William, *Agenda*, 24:3-4, Autumn-Winter 1996-97: 5 [Editorial].
Crossley-Holland, Kevin, *The Language of Yes* (Enitharmon Press, London, 1996) [Acknowledgements].
As the Poet Said..., edited by Tony Curtis (Poetry Ireland/Eigse Eireann, Dublin, 1997): 18 [Quotation].

Falck, Colin, *American and British Verse in the Twentieth Century: The Poetry that Matters* (Ashgate, Aldershot, 2004).

Görtschacher, Wolfgang, *Little Magazine Profiles: The Little Magazines in Great Britain, 1939-1993* (University of Salzburg, Salzburg, 1993): 127-128, 567-568.

Harris-Hendriks, Jean, Dora Black and Tony Kaplan, *When Father Kills Mother: Guiding Children through Trauma and Grief* (Routledge, London and New York, 1993; Routledge, London and Philadelphia, 1999): heading chapter 5 [Two lines quoted from 'The Old Path'].

Unsigned [Philip Hoy], 'A Note on Ian Hamilton', *Ian Hamilton in Conversation with Dan Jacobson* (Between the Lines, London, 2002): 15.

Jacobson, Dan, *Ian Hamilton in Conversation with Dan Jacobson* (Between the Lines, London, 2002): 182, 184, 190 [The last under 'John Surple', a pen-name].

John, Roland, *A Beginner's Guide to the Cantos of Ezra Pound* (University of Salzburg/Hippopotamus Press, Salzburg, Austria, 1995) [Acknowledgements].

Selected Letters of Philip Larkin, edited by Anthony Thwaite (Faber and Faber, London, 1992 / Farrar, Straus, Giroux, New York, 1993): 468 [Letter to John Wain, 10 December 1972].

Envoi Book of Quotes on Poetry, edited by Anne Lewis-Smith and selected by Clifford Hammond (Envoi Poets, Newport, Dyfed, 1991): 24.

Miller, Karl, *Seamus Heaney in Conversation with Karl Miller* (Between the Lines, London, 2000): 103 [Critics section].

Milne, W. S., *An Introduction to Geoffrey Hill* (Bellew, London, 1998): 10.

Mutis, Álvaro, *Abdul Bashur, soñador de navíos* (Grupo Editorial Norma, Barcelona, 1991 / Ediciones Siruela, Madrid, 1991) [Epigraph: last two lines of 'He addresses himself to Reflection' from 'Mirrors, Windows', a sonnet sequence in *Earth Light*].

Navrozov, Andrei, 'What Price Literature Now?', *The Times*, 3 February 1989.

Oxley, William, 'Checklist of Long Poems', *The Long Poem Group Newsletter 1*, May 1995: 3 [Listing].

Pursglove, Glyn, 'Poetry Comment', *Acumen*, 34, May 1999: 102.

Silkin, Jon, *Out of Battle: The Poetry of the Great War* (Oxford University Press, London, 1972): 211.

Wade, Stephen, 'Keeping Quiet' (Bosun Press, Lincs., 2003) [Dedication, inside cover, with edited verbatim remark by PD].

Uncollected Prose (excluding *Agenda* Pieces)

'The Poet and Society', *Isis*, 24 January 1962: 16-17.
'Robert Lowell', *Isis*, 14 June 1962: 21 [Review].
'Graves as Critic and Essayist', *Isis*, 20 June 1962 [Review].
'Poetry: In ISIS and Oxford', *Isis*, 23 January 1963.
'Romantic Paradox by C. G. Clarke', *Isis*, 1963: 26 [Review].
'Contemporary Amedican (sic) Poetry', *Isis*, 6 February 1963: 29 [Review; Selected and introduced by Donald Hall].
'Experience and Experiencing', *Isis*, 6 March 1963: 18, 20, 23 [Review].
'From Literature and from Life', *Times Literary Supplement*, 3222, 28 November 1963: 995 [Daniel Hughes, *Waking in a Tree*; James Wright, *The Branch Will Not Break*].
'Rhythm and Beat', *Times Literary Supplement*, 3227, 2 January 1964: 10 [*Penguin Modern Poets, vol IV*: David Holbrook, Christopher Middleton, David Wevill; *Penguin Modern Poets, Vol. V*: Gregory Corso, Lawrence Ferlinghetti, Allen Ginsburg].
'A Moderate Line-up', *Times Literary Supplement*, 3261, 27 August 1964: 766 [D. M. Thomas, *Personal and Possessive*; Peter Russell, *Visions and Ruins*; Geoffrey Sutton, *Half a Loaf*].
'R.I.P.', *Times Literary Supplement*, 3272, 12 November 1964: 1023 [*Fifteen Poems for William Shakespeare*, edited by Eric Walter White].
'Quartet', *Times Literary Supplement*, 3302, 10 June 1965: 476 [Terence Hards, *As It Was*; Norman MacCaig, *Measures*; A. L. Hendriks, *On This Mountain*; Philip Callow, *The Real Life*].
'His Because the Same', *The Listener*, 8 December 1966.
'Only for the Fanatics', *Tribune*, 7 June 1968 [*A Portrait of the Artist as a Young Man*].
'Generosity and Gaiety', *Tribune*, 16 August 1968 [*Collected Poems of Theodore Roethke*].
'A Persuasive Voice', *The Times*, 19 April 1969 [Saturday Review].
'The Subjective Classicist', *Art and Artists*, 4:3, June 1969: 12-15 [Ben Nicholson].

'A Society in Conflict', *Tribune*, 13 June 1969.
'Imagination and Violence', *The Times*, 6 September 1969 [Saturday Review].
'Greene's Gay Novel', *Tribune*, 21 November 1969.
'Commitment', *Art and Artists*, April 1970 [Jean-Paul Sartre].
'A Brush with Words', *Art and Artists*, May 1970: 24-27 [David Storey and David Mercer].
'Greene in Collection', *Tribune*, 22 May 1970.
'The Limits of Language', *Tribune*, 5 June 1970.
'A Starter-Off of Crazes', *Tribune*, 23 October 1970.
'Three Poets: Can Belief and Form Come in a Bag of Tricks?', *Saturday Review* (USA), 55:28, 8 July 1972: 57-58.
'Partisan', *New Statesman*, 17 November 1972: 730.
'*Agenda*: The Problems of a Small Magazine', *Greater London Arts Association Newsletter*, April 1974.
'Proximities', *Delta*, 55, December 1976: 12-14 [*The Complete Poems of Thomas Hardy*].
'The Drama of Reason', *Canto* (Andover, Mass.), 3:1, 1979: 166-178 [Geoffrey Hill].
[Review], South Eastern Arts Council Magazine, 1980: 50 [Gabriel Josipovici, *The Echo Chamber*].
'Bunting and Villon', *Paideuma: A Journal Devoted to Ezra Pound Scholarship*, 9:1, Spring 1980: 101-107.
'Inconsequences', *Poetry Review*, 70:1-2, September 1980: 73-77.
[Reviews], South Eastern Arts Council Magazine, December 1982: 118-119 [Alistair Fowler, *From the Domain of Arnheim*; Richard Kell, *The Broken Circle*].
Note on 'Meditation Down the Wards', *Footnote* (Schools Poetry Association Publication), 50, 1985.
Note on 'Patient in a Ward', *Footnote* (Schools Poetry Association Publication), 51, 1985.
'The Line', *Footnotes Magazine* (Schools' Poetry Association), 3, 1987: unnumbered [Footnote on poem by PD].
'Forging Laforgue', *Poetry Society Newsletter*, January 1987.
Surple, Peter (pseud.), *Outposts*, 152, Spring 1987: 53-55 [A. S. J. Tessimond, *The Collected Poems*; Wyatt Prunty, *What Women Know, What Men Believe*; Peter Scupham, *Out Late*].
'Editorial', in *Agenda* Supplement of *Scripsi*, 4:4, September 1987: 187.
'The New Freedom of Rhyme', *Chronicles*, 11:10, October 1987: 16-18 [Revised in *Outposts*, 168, Spring 1991: 3-8].
'On translating Baudelaire', *Acumen*, 6, October 1987: 74.
Outposts, 156, Spring 1988: 60-61 [Robinson Jeffers, *Selected Poems*, edited by Colin Falck].
'Réflexions sur la traduction', *La Poésie française au tournant des années 80*, edited by Philippe Delaveau (Librairie José Corti, Paris, 1988): 224 [Translation not by PD].
'Adjudicator's Report on the 1987 Competition', *Outposts*, 157, Summer 1988: 55-56 [See also editor's note, page 71].
'Note sur la rime', *Le Courrier* (Brussels), 182, April-June 1989: 27-28.
'Dan Dant', *Acumen*, 10, October 1989: 68-69.
'The Arkansas Testament', *Outposts*, 171, Winter 1991: 42-45 [Derek Walcott].
'Dyment, Clifford', 'Rhyme', 'Tessimond, A.S.J.', entries in *The Oxford Companion to Twentieth Century Poetry*, edited by Ian Hamilton (Oxford University Press, Oxford, 1994): 142, 450-451, 536.
'The Soft Idiot Softly', *20-20: Making Waves, 1991-1994* (Making Waves, Guildford, 1994): 13-23.
'Doctor Honoris Causa, Marius Kociejowski', *Outposts*, 178, 1994: 65-66.
'Out of Danger by James Fenton', *Acumen*, 19, April 1994: 93-95.
[Reviews], *The Use of English*, 45:3, Summer 1994: 280-285.
'*What and Who* by C. H. Sisson; *The Red-headed Pupil*, by Jeffrey Wainwright', *Acumen*, 20, October 1994: 94-96.
'Of Love, Time and Places: Selected Poems, Charles Madge', *Outposts*, 180-181, 1995: 155-156.
'The Sonnet Form', *The Swansea Review*, 14, 1995: 15-20 [Sonnet Issue].
'A Calendar of Modern Poetry – P. N. Review', *The Use of English*, 46:3, Summer 1995: 270-273.
'Anthology Choices', *Acumen*, 24, January 1996: 40.
'Penguin Modern Poets', *The Use of English*, 47:2, Spring 1996: 186-189.
'Nude Studies in French Verse', *In Other Words* (Journal of the Translators' Association), Summer 1996: 24-28.
'A Translator Who Understands His Language', *Stand*, 37:4, Autumn 1996: 68-70 [Editorial].
'The State of Modernism', *The Dark Horse*, 5, Summer 1997: 52-57.
'The Ideal Introduction to the Impossible Anthology', *Acumen*, 32, September 1998: 11-15.

'College Daze', *Another Round at the Pillars: Essays, Poems & Reflections on Ian Hamilton*, edited by David Harsent (Cargo Press, Tregarne, Cornwall, 1999): 43-53 [Festschrift for Ian Hamilton's Sixtieth Birthday].
'Language in War and Rebellion', *Poetry London Newsletter*, 32, Spring 1999: 22-23.
'Oxford in Verse', *Oxford Today*, Trinity Term, 1999: 27 [*Oxford in Verse*, compiled by Glyn Pursglove and Alistair Ricketts].
'Laforgue Revisited', *In Other Words* (Journal of the Translators' Association), 13-14, Autumn-Winter 1999-2000: 40-45.
'Enoch Soames: Eldertorial', *Acumen*, 37, 2000: 90-91.
'Rhyme and Reason', *La Tribune Internationale des Langues Vivantes* (France), 2001: 26-33 [Machine translation of verse].
'Peter Dale's Comments', *Writers' Forum*, 7:6, December 2001-January 2002: 51 [On 'Half-Light'].
'Crise de Vers', translated by Maryse Hovens, *Balises: Cahiers de Poétique des Archives & Musée de la Littérature* (Brussels), 3-4, 2002-03: 213-222.
'A Round-up', *The London Magazine*, October-November 2003: 89-93.

BIOGRAPHICAL PIECES

'William Cookson', *The New College Record*, 2002, May 2003: 47-49 [Obituary].

LETTERS TO PRESS

'Trade Names', *Times Literary Supplement*, 3452, 25 April 1968: 438.
'Browning's Syllabics', *Listener*, 19 April 1970.
'Poetic Lament' [co-signed with William Cookson], *The Guardian*, 9 February 1973.
Agenda, 11:4-12:1, Autumn-Winter 1973-74: 159 [Reply to letter by Robert Lowell].
Agenda, 17:1, Spring 1979: 114-115 [Reply to Peter Jay, regarding Sappho].
'A Plaque for Pound', *The Times*, December 1988 [Signatory to a group letter instigated by Dr Alistair Niven].
Stand, 38:4, Autumn 1997 [On rime, reply to James Sutherland-Smith].
Acumen, 46, May 2003: 88 [On Between the Lines publication of Hamilton interview].

EDITORIAL: *AGENDA*

Agenda, 10:4-11:1, Autumn-Winter 1972-73: 3 [Special Issue on Rhythm; With other editorial selections: 'Tradition Answers Back', 'Problems of Prosodists and Rhythm Rulers': 59-67].
Agenda, 11:4-12:1, Autumn-Winter 1973-74: 102 [David Jones Special Issue].
Agenda, 12:2, Summer 1974: 3-5.
'The Oddest Profession in the World', *Agenda*, 12:3, Autumn 1974: 3-5.
Agenda, 12:4-13:1, Winter-Spring 1975: 3, 88-90 [First part; Books Received].
Agenda, 14:3, Autumn 1976: 3-5; 29; 96-99 [Special Issue on Criticism].
Agenda, 14:4-15:1, April 1977: 3 [New English and American Poems – An Anthology].
Agenda, 15:4, Winter 1977-78: 3 [French Poetry Issue].
Agenda, 18:4-19:1, Winter-Spring 1981: 3-5 [Verse Drama Issue].
Agenda, 22:4-23:1, Winter-Spring 1983-84: 3 [Stanley Burnshaw Issue].
Agenda supplement, *Scripsi*, 4:4, September 1987: 187.
Agenda, 27:3, Autumn 1989: 3-5; 22-25 [State of Poetry Issue].
Agenda, 28:2, Summer 1990: 3-4 [Creditorial].
Agenda, 28:3, Autumn 1990: 5-6 [Meditorial; Anthology of New Poems].
Agenda, 28:4, Winter 1991: 13-15 [With preliminary note; A Survey on Rhyme Issue].
Agenda, 29:4, Winter 1991 [Roy Fuller, International Issue].
Agenda, 31:2, Summer 1993: 3-4 [With addition by William Cookson; The Sixties Issue].
Agenda, 33:1, Spring 1995: 3-4; 5-6; 39-42 [With introduction to 'Press Gangs' articles; *Agenda* Editions entry, 'The War of Words' Selection; The Seventies Issue].

CRITICAL PIECES IN AGENDA

Agenda, 2:7-8, May-June 1962: 12-17 [*The New Poetry*, edited by A. Alvarez].
Agenda, 2:7-8, May-June 1962: 17-19 [*Selected Poems of Thom Gunn and Ted Hughes*].
Agenda, 2:7-8, May-June 1962: 21-25 [Thom Gunn, *Fighting Terms, My Sad Captains*].
'Graves, Wilbur, Edith Sitwell, Vernon Watkins', *Agenda*, 2:11-12, April 1963: 19-23.
Agenda, 3:1, August-September 1963 [*A Group Anthology*, edited by Lucie-Smith; Review in verse].
Agenda, 3:3, January 1964: 19-23 [*The Collected Poems of Wilfred Owen; New Lines II*].
Agenda, 3:5, September 1964: 28-30 [e. e. cummings, *73 Poems*; *Selected Poems of Douglas*, edited by Ted Hughes; Philip Larkin, *The Whitsun Weddings*].
Agenda, 3:5, September 1964: 34-35 [Jon Silkin, *Flower Poems*; Ken Smith, *Eleven Poems*; Geoffrey Hill, *Preghiere*].
'The Review Pamphlets: Ian Hamilton, Michael Fried, Colin Falck', *Agenda*, 4:1, April-May 1965: 49-52.
Agenda, 4:1, April-May 1965: 53-58 [Edward Lucie-Smith, *Confessions & Histories*; David Wevill, *Birth of a Shark*].
'O Honey bees come build ...', *Agenda*, 4:3-4, Summer 1966: 49-54 [Sylvia Plath, *Ariel*].
Agenda, 4:3-4, Summer 1966: 76-78 [Robert Lowell, *For the Union Dead*].
Agenda, 4:5-6, Autumn 1966: 61-63 [Seamus Heaney, *Death of a Naturalist*; Thomas Kinsella, *Wormwood*; Jon Silkin, *New and Selected Poems*].
'Geoffrey Hill, Roy Fuller', *Agenda*, 6:3-4, Autumn-Winter 1968: 150-151 [Double Translation Issue].
'Translating *Beowulf*', *Agenda*, 7:2, Spring 1969: 68-69.
'Auden, Lowell, Snodgrass, Stafford', *Agenda*, 7:2, Spring 1969: 79-81.
'The Pound/Joyce Letters', *Agenda*, 7:2, Spring 1969: 86.
'Self-Condemned', *Agenda*, 7:3-8:1, Autumn-Winter 1969-70: 31-36 [Wyndham Lewis Special Issue].
'Revenge for Love', *Agenda*, 7:3-8:1, Autumn-Winter 1969-70: 71-77 [Wyndham Lewis Special Issue].
'Between the Lines: The Poetry of Ian Hamilton', *Agenda*, 9:1, Winter 1971: 38-44 [Ian Hamilton, *The Visit*].
'Slithy Tome', *Agenda*, 9:1, Winter 1971: 52-61 [John Berryman, *His Toy, His Dream, His Rest: 308 Dream Songs*].
'Pen and Ink' [under pseudonym, J. Hayles]), *Agenda*, 9:1, Winter 1971: 62-63 [*The Survival of Poetry: A Contemporary Survey*, edited by Martin Dodsworth].
'Shorter Notices: New Collections', 'Paperbacks and Penguins', 'Pamphlets', *Agenda*, 9:1, Winter 1971: 71-77.
'Crow', *Agenda*, 9:2-3, Spring-Summer 1971: 97-101.
'Where all the ladders start ...', *Agenda*, 9:4-10:1, Autumn-Winter 1971-72: 3-13 [W. B. Yeats].
Agenda, 9:4-10:1, Autumn-Winter 1971-72: 144-145 [*23 British Poets*, edited by John Matthias].
'Kids' Stuff', *Agenda*, 9:4-10:1, Autumn-Winter 1971-72: 147-149 [George MacBeth, *Collected Poems*].
Agenda, 10:4-11:1, Autumn-Winter 1972-73: 14-16 [Answer to Rhythm Questionnaire].
'The Waste Land', *Agenda*, 10:4-11:1, Autumn-Winter 1972-73: 155-157 [Discusses the facsimile version of Eliot's poem].
'Fortuitous Form', *Agenda*, 11:2-3, Spring-Summer 1973: 73-87 [Robert Lowell, *History; For Lizzie and Harriet; Dolphin*].
'Problems of the Short Poem', *Agenda*, 11:4-12:1, Autumn-Winter 1973-74: 149-154 [Samuel Menashe and Michael Fried].
Agenda, 12:3, Autumn 1974: 32-39 [Stanley Burnshaw, *The Seamless Web*; Romanian Issue].
'Books Received', *Agenda*, 12:3, Autumn 1974: 58-61 [Romanian Issue; Desmond Graham, *Keith Douglas, 1920-1944: A Biography*; Jon Silkin, *The Principle of Water*; Stephen Miller, Elizabeth Maslen, Kit Wright (Treble Poets: 1); *Pope*, selected by Peter Levi].
'Books Received', *Agenda*, 12:4-13:1, Winter-Spring 1975: 88-90 [Edgell Rickword; John Clare; Patrick Kavanagh; Verlaine in translation].
'Regionalism: Three Overlooked Poets'[under pseudonym, F. Giles], *Agenda*, 13:2, Summer 1975: 75-77 [Endpaper].
'Reconsiderations: *Articulate Energy*', *Agenda*, 14:3, Autumn 1976: 85-86 [Special Issue on Criticism].
Spoof answer to questionnaire [under pseudonym, Enoch Soames], *Agenda*, 14:3, Autumn 1976: 29 [Special Issue on Criticism].
'Three Critics: One Poem' [under pseudonym, S. James], *Agenda*, 14:3, Autumn 1976: 93-95 [Special

Issue on Criticism].
Giles, F. (pseud.), 'Critic at Work', *Agenda*, 14:3, Autumn 1976: 96-99 [Special Issue on Criticism].
'Going Public', *Agenda*, 15:2-3, Summer-Autumn 1977: 142-146 [Stanley Burnshaw, *Mirages: Travel Notes in the Promised Land*].
'*Gaudete* by Ted Hughes', *Agenda*, 15:2-3, Summer-Autumn 1977: 153-156 [Review in verse].
'Basil Bunting and the Quonk and Groggle School of Poetry', *Agenda*, 16:1, 1978: 55-65 [Basil Bunting Special Issue].
'Poetic Licence', *Agenda*, 16:3-4, Autumn-Winter 1978-79: 69-72.
'*Instigations* – Ezra Pound and Remy De Gourmont', *Agenda*, 17:3-4-18:1, Winter-Spring 1979-80: 284 [Ezra Pound Special Issue].
Agenda, 19:2-3, Summer-Winter 1981-82: 88-89 [Christopher Hampton, *A Cornered Freedom*; J. P. Taylor, *The Hollow Places*; Randall Jarrell, *Kipling, Auden & Co*].
Surple, John (pseud.), 'Andrew Waterman: *Out for the Elements*', *Agenda*, 19:4-20:1, Spring 1982: 105-107.
'The Poems of Stanley Burnshaw', *Agenda*, 21:4-22:1, Winter-Spring 1983-84: 11-19.
'Prose Rhythm and Oral Tradition', *Agenda*, 23:1-2, Spring-Summer 1985: 87-92 [T.S. Eliot Special Issue].
'Books received', *Agenda*, 26:3, Autumn 1988: 77-81.
Agenda, 27:3, Autumn 1989: 15-17 [Answer to the circular, The State of Poetry Issue].
'Book [sic] Received', *Agenda*, 28:4, Winter 1991: 93-97.
'Some Thoughts on Rhyme in *The Mystery of the Charity of Charles Péguy*', *Agenda*, 30:1-2, Spring-Summer 1992: 32-34.
Surple, John (pseud.), 'Ian Hamilton', *Agenda*, 31:2, Summer 1993: 107-111 [The Sixties Issue].
'The New Poetry', *Agenda*, 31:3, Autumn 1993: 134-138.
Agenda, 32:3-4, Autumn-Winter 1994-95: 271-274 [Laura Riding, *Selected Poems*; W.H. Auden, *Juvenilia*; A Tribute to Peter Russell Issue].
'Two New Little Poetry Magazines: *The New Poetry Quarterly*', *Agenda*, 32:3-4, Autumn-Winter 1994-95: 327.
Agenda, 35:3, Autumn 1997: 119-121 [Michael Hamburger, *The Truth of Poetry*].
Agenda, 37:1, Summer 1999: 81 [John Fuller, *W. H. Auden: A Commentary*].

QUESTIONNAIRES MADE FOR *AGENDA*

Rhythm, *Agenda*, 10:4-11:1, Autumn-Winter 1972-73: 7-8.
Supplement on Rhythm: From America, *Agenda*, 11:2-3, Spring-Summer 1973: 38-39.
Special Issue on Criticism: Questionnaire, *Agenda*, 14:3, Autumn 1976: 5-6.
State of Poetry, circular of quotations on poetry, *Agenda*, 27:3, Autumn 1989: 3-5.
A Survey on Rhyme: Editorial Note and *Agenda* Questionnaire, *Agenda*, 28:4, Winter 1991: 5-7.

SQUIBS, PARODIES AND SATIRES

'The Lake Isle', *Agenda*, 3:5, September 1964: 19.
'Just a Swing at Everyone: Mongolia, Rue Fuller'; 'Oxford, D. N. Avidhearts'; 'Duobog, Patter Dull'; 'Saving Up, Inane Hammertone'; *Agenda*, 9:4-10:1, Autumn-Winter 1971-72: 150-152 [Yeats/Montale Issue].
'Printer's Pie', *Agenda*, 10:4-11:1, Autumn-Winter 1972-73: inside back cover.
'Virtue', *Agenda*, 19:2-3, Summer-Autumn 1981: 144.
'The New Testament of Jean de Calais', *Agenda*, 19:2-3, Summer 1982: 151-156.
'Wat the Dunderhead', *Agenda*, 23:1-2, Spring-Summer 1985: 180 [T. S. Eliot Issue].
'The Vice Salacious', *Agenda*, 23:1-2, Spring-Summer 1985: 184 [T. S. Eliot Issue].
Giles, F. (pseud.), 'Of Spoken Mages', *Agenda*, 24:1, Spring 1986: 78 [Craig Raine, *Rich*].
'The State of Poetry' [under pseudonym, Paddy O'Ffandish] *Agenda*, 27:3, Autumn 1989: 80-81, 15-17 [Rhyming response to the circulated questions, The State of Poetry Issue].
'Love in a Life', *Agenda*, 29:1-2, Spring-Summer 1991: 119 [Long Poems Double Issue].
'Co-Editor's Note', *Agenda*, 32:3-4, Autumn-Winter 1994-95: 5.

EDITORIAL: *OXFORD TODAY*

'Living Oxford Poets: Unconquered Flame: Elizabeth Jennings', 11:3, Trinity Term, 1999: 27 [Head-note].
'Living Oxford Poets: Donald Hall', 12:1, Michaelmas Term, 1999: 56 [Head-note and selection; headnote to verse by Ian Blake].
'Living Oxford Poets: Michael Thwaites', 12:2, Hilary Term, 2000: 56 [Head-note and selection].
'J. C. Hall', 12:3, Trinity Term, 2000: 55 [Head-note and selection].
'Oxford Poets: Reaching a Peak', 13:1, Michaelmas Term, 2000: 31 [A. Alvarez; Head-note and selection].
'Oxford Poetry: Michael Fried', 13:2, Hilary Term, 2001: 49 [Head-note and selection].
'Oxford Poetry: Mairi MacInnes', 13:3, Trinity Term, 2001: 31 [Head-note and selection].
'Oxford Poetry: Ian Hamilton', 14:1, Michaelmas Term, 2001: 54 [Head-note and selection].
'Oxford Poetry: Pauline Stainer', 14:2, Hilary Term, 2002: 39 [Head-note and selection].
'Oxford Poetry: Dom Moraes', 14:3, Trinity Term, 2002: 53 [Head-note and selection].
'Oxford Poetry: Antony Dunn, David Hartnett, Jem Poster', 15:1, Michaelmas Term, 2002: 57 [Head-notes and selection].
'Oxford poetry: Duncan Forbes', 15:2, Hilary Term, 2003: 55 [Head-note and selection].
'Oxford poetry: Hilary Davies, Elizabeth Garret, Jenny Joseph', 15:3, Trinity Term, 2003: 35 [Head-notes and selection].
'Oxford poetry: Michael Hamburger, John Whitworth, David Clarke', 16:1, Michaelmas Term, 2003: 35 [Head-notes and selection].
'Oxford poetry: Alan Brownjohn, Wendy Cope, Lawrence Sail', 16:2, Hilary Term, 2004 [Head-notes and selection].
'Oxford poetry: Ian Parks, Anthony Thwaite, Sarah Wardle', 16:3, Trinity Term, 2004: 35 [Selection of poems and headnote on Parks].
'Oxford poetry: C. J. Driver, Chris Mann, Ian Morris', Michaelmas Term, 2004: 27 [Head-notes and selection].

SECONDARY MATERIAL

SPECIAL DALE ISSUES OF MAGAZINES

Agenda, 13:3, Autumn 1975 [Sisson, Hill, Hamburger, Dale].
Agenda, 26:2, Summer 1988 [Peter Dale Issue].
Outposts, 156, Spring 1988: 50-78 [The Poetry of Peter Dale].

REVIEWS OF BOOKS OF POEMS

WALK FROM THE HOUSE (1962)

Anon. [Horne, Professor Colin J.], 'Pathway to Parnassus', *Times Literary Supplement*, 3204, 26 July 1963: 557.
Alvarez, A., 'New poetry in paperback', *The Observer*, 13 January 1963 [Weekend Review].
Cookson, William, *Agenda*, 2:11-12, March-April 1963: 13-17 [Rev. of four Fantasy Press Poets; Reprinted, with excisions, in *Agenda*, 39:4, Summer 2003: 118-120 (Celebratory Issue for William Cookson)].
Falck, Colin, 'The Lyrical Man', *The Review*, 5, 1963: 40-44.
Kaufman, Wallace, *Isis*, 23 January 1963 [Rev. of four Fantasy Press Poets].

THE STORMS (1968)

Anon. [Thwaite, Anthony], 'Verse and Versatility', *Times Literary Supplement*, 3442, 15 February 1968:

155.
Brace, Keith, 'Private Poetry Fights Back', *The Birmingham Post*, 30 November 1968.
Byrom, Bill, 'America: English Groundswell in the East', *The Times*, 4 May 1968 [Saturday Review].
Cushman, Jerome, *Library Journal*, August 1968: 2881.
Dodsworth, Martin, *The Listener*, 1 February 1968.
Gray, Edmund, 'Peter Dale and the Imagination', *Agenda*, 6:2, Spring 1968: 75-80.
Hamilton, Ian, 'Bringing Out the Worst', *The Observer*, 11 February 1968.
Jones, Brian, 'Poetry', *London Magazine*, May 1968: 75-77.
Kennedy, X. J., 'The Devalued Estate', *Poetry* (Chicago), July 1969.
Robson, Jeremy, 'Exciting Poetry', *Tribune*, [early 1968].
Symons, Julian, 'MacSpaunday', *New Statesman*, 1 March 1968: 276.
Unsigned, 'Familiar Scenes in Poet's New Volume', *Surrey Herald*, 26 January 1968.
Unsigned, 'The Storms', *The Writer's Review*, 5:1, 1968.
Wright, Caroline, 'After "The Storms"', *Agenda*, 26:2, Summer 1988: 95 [Parody].

MORTAL FIRE (1970)

Ehrenpreis, Irvin, 'Moments of Suffocation', *Times Literary Supplement*, 3566, 2 July 1970: 703.
Cookson, William, 'Notes on the Poetry of Peter Dale', *Agenda*, 8:3-4, Autumn-Winter 1970: 89-95.
Eagleton, Terry, 'New Poetry', *Stand*, 11, 1970: 77-78.
Fuller, John, 'Porter's Complaint', *The Listener*, 24 December 1970.
Jay, David, 'Suburban Sensation', *Times Educational Supplement*, 18 September 1970.
Porter, Peter, 'In the Bosom of the Family', *London Magazine*, September 1970: 70.
Hamilton, Ian, 'A Matter of Balance', *Observer*, 19 July 1970.
Robson, Jeremy, 'Painted on a Large Canvas', *Tribune*, 11 September 1970.
Smith, John, 'Abroad Thoughts from Home', *Poetry Review*, 1970: 363-365.
Wall, Stephen, 'Letting It Happen', *The Review*, 23, September-November 1970: 61-65.
Wright, Caroline and Helen Widdess, 'Thinking of Having a Baby', *Agenda*, 19:2-3, Summer-Autumn 1981: 143 [Parody].

MORTAL FIRE: SELECTED POEMS (1976)

Anon., 'Dale, Peter, *Mortal Fire*', *Choice*, October 1976: 978.
Anon., *The Booklist*, 15 June 1976.
Anon., *Poetry Wales*, 12:2, Autumn 1976.
Bedford, William, 'The Poetry of Ordinariness', *Agenda*, 14:4-15:1, April 1977: 94-109.
Bedford, William, 'Fathers and Sons: Peter Dale's *Mortal Fire*', *The Southern Review*, Winter 1979: 238-241.
Crowhurst, Kenneth, *Agenda*, 13:4-14:1, Winter-Spring 1976: 133-136 [Letter to the editor; Response from Grey Gowrie].
Davie, Donald, 'Father's Story', *The Listener*, 28 October 1976.
Dunn, Douglas, *Encounter*, November 1976: 78.
Eisiminger, Skip, 'Peter Dale, *Mortal Fire*', *Green River Review*, January 1977.
Mole, John, 'Man is a Landscape', *Times Literary Supplement*, 3890, 1 October 1976: 1235.
Oxley, William, *The Littack Supplement*, October 1976: 2.
Portis, Rowe, 'Dale, Peter, *Mortal Fire*', *Library Journal*, August 1976: 1640.
Schreiber, Jan, 'Peter Dale's *Mortal Fire*', *Canto* (Andover, Mass.), 1:1, Spring 1977: 133-137.
Wade, Stephen, '"No Narrow English Voice": Peter Dale's *The Going*', *Agenda*, 26:2, Summer 1988: 56-62 [Specifically discusses 'The Going', a sequence in *Mortal Fire*; Peter Dale Issue].
Wright, David, 'Most Unexpectedly', *Poetry Nation Review*, 3, Spring 1977: 61.

CROSS CHANNEL (1977)

Graham, Desmond, 'Notwithstanding Imagism, or the Limits of Austerity', *Stand*, 19:1, 1977-78: 74-80.
Mrosovsky, Kitty, 'Keith Bosley's Mallarmé', *Agenda*, 15:4, Winter 1977-78: 66 [French issues].

ONE ANOTHER: A SONNET SEQUENCE (1978)

Bedford, William, 'Narrative and Epiphany: Peter Dale's *One Another*', *Agenda*, 17:1, Spring 1979: 101-106.
Eagleton, Terry, 'New Poetry', *Stand*, 20:1, 1978-79: 74-79.
Fisher, Emma, 'The Nature of Imagery', *PNR*, 6:3, 1980: 57-59.
Johnson, Anthony L., 'Reviews', *Littack*, 1980: 10.
Love, Tim, ''The End of the Line for Modern Poetry', *Acumen*, 29, 1997: 30.
Matthews, John, '*Agenda* Basil Bunting Special Issue, Volume 16, No.1', *Labrys*, 1980.
Matthews, John, '*One Another*: a sonnet sequence, Peter Dale', *Labrys*, 1980.
Milne, W. S., '"Not Just A Case of Words": Peter Dale's *One Another*', *Agenda*, 26:2, Summer 1988: 49-54 [Peter Dale Issue].
Milne, W. S., 'Sonnet Boom', *Sunday Times*, 21 January 1996 [Letter to the editor regarding the state of the sonnet form].
Prunty, Wyatt, 'Reciprocals', *The Southern Review*, 17:3, July 1981: 634-641.
Sail, Lawrence, 'Working the Middle Ground', *Poetry Review*, 69:2, December 1979: 68-69.
Shepherd, W. G., 'Peter Dale's *One Another*', *The Many Review*, 6, January 1992: 21-27.
Shepherd, W. G., 'Solipsism Transcended', *Agenda*, 33:1, Spring 1995: 89-95 [Later version of above; Seventies Issue].
Stevenson Anne, 'Being Happy', *The Listener*, 15 March 1979: 386.
Tibble, Anne, *Outposts*, 123, Winter 1979: 28-29.
Thomas, D. M., 'The Habits of Love', *Times Literary Supplement*, 3992, 6 October 1978: 1125.
Tunnicliffe, Stephen, 'A New Sonnet Sequence', *The Use of English*, Autumn 1978: 50.

TOO MUCH OF WATER: POEMS 1976-82 (1983)

Annwn, David, *Labrys*, 10 May 1984:195-196.
Barker, Jonathan, 'Attendant Shadows', *PNR*, Autumn 1984: 68-69.
Bedford, William, '"Redolence Returning, Touched with Brine"', *Agenda*, 22:3-4, Autumn 1984-Winter 1985: 71-77.
Haslehurst, Martin, *Anglo-Welsh Review*, 76, 1984: 93-95.
Loveday, John, *Outposts*, 156, Spring 1988: 65-67.
Mackinnon, Lachlan, 'Preening and Glazing', *Times Literary Supplement*, 4243, 27 July 1984: 838.
Wade, Stephen, 'Too Much of Water', *Agenda*, 22:3-4, Autumn 1984-Winter 1985: 68-70.

A SET OF DARTS: EPIGRAMS FOR THE NINETIES (1990)

F. C., 'Books Received', *Outposts*, 168, Spring 1991: 54.

EARTH LIGHT (1991)

Bedford William, 'Who Says Does Not Know', *Agenda*, 26:2, Summer 1988: 29-37 [Specifically discusses 'Mirrors, Windows', a sonnet sequence in *Earth Light*; Peter Dale Issue].
Bedford, William, '*Earth Light*, Peter Dale', *Agenda*, 29:4, Winter 1991: 76-79.
Kennedy, David, 'Beyond Local Borders', *PNR*, 19:3, January-February 1993: 61-62.
Pain, Margaret, 'The Working of Words', *Orbis*, 1992: 17-18.
Salzman, Eva, 'The Formal and the Fast-Food', *Times Literary Supplement*, 4657, 3 July 1992: 28.
Shepherd, W.G., '*Earth Light*', *Outposts*, 171, Winter 1991: 76-80.
Wainwright, Eddie, 'Alpha to Omega', *Envoi*, 1992: 61-64.
Zaller, Robert, *The Texas Review*, 14:1-2, Summer 1993: 128-130.

EDGE TO EDGE: NEW AND SELECTED POEMS (1996)

Brownjohn, Alan, 'The Mark of the Mature', *The Sunday Times* (Books), 26 January 1997.

Griffiths, Ted, 'Edge to Edge: New and Selected Poems', *Outposts*, 184, Autumn 1998: 6-13.
Kilby, Michael, 'The Poetry of Peter Dale', *Agenda*, 35:1, Spring 1997: 102-107.
Lucas, John, *Stand*, 39:2, Spring 1998: 83-84.
Wade, Stephen, *Acumen*, 33, January 1998: 84-86.

DA CAPO: A SEQUENCE (1997)

Pursglove, Glyn, 'Poetry Comment', *Acumen*, 31, May 1998: 106.

UNDER THE BREATH (2002)

Gahagan, Judy, 'Peter Dale: Under the Breath', *Ambit*, 175, January 2004: 54-55.
John, Roland, 'Peter Dale: Under the Breath', *Envoi*, October 2003: 114-115.
Kenney, Morgan, 'In Search of Poetry', *Writers' Forum*, 7:6, December 2001-January 2002: 51-52 [On 'Half-Light'].
Lomas, Herbert, 'Sliding Carpets', *The London Magazine*, June-July 2003: 106-110.
Milne, W. S., 'Insidious Mastery', *Acumen*, 46, Spring 2003: 99-106.
Milne, W. S., *Stand*, 5:2, September 2003: 61-63.
Pursglove, Glyn, 'Poetry Comment', *Acumen*, 45, January 2003: 114.
Robinson, Peter, 'Survivor's Art', *The Guardian*, 19 April 2003: 25.

ONE ANOTHER (2002)

Robinson, Peter, 'Survivor's Art', *The Guardian*, 19 April 2003: 25.
Schreiber, Jan, 'The Mystery of Her', *Edge City Review*, 6:3 (No. 19), March 2004.

REVIEWS OF OTHER BOOKS

MICHAEL HAMBURGER IN CONVERSATION WITH PETER DALE (1998)

Pursglove, Glyn, 'Pilcrows', *Swansea Review*, 18, Spring 1999: 177-179.
Pybus, Rodney, 'Briefs and Shorts', *Stand*, 40:1, Winter 1998: 34.
Thorpe, Adam, 'Peculiar Darkness', *Poetry Review*, 88, Winter 1998-99: 49-50. [Round-up review of various Michael Hamburger books].

AN INTRODUCTION TO RHYME (1998)

Oxley, William, 'Mediating for the Reader', *Acumen*, 33, January 1999: 91-92.

ANTHONY THWAITE IN CONVERSATION WITH PETER DALE AND IAN HAMILTON (1999)

Crotty, Patrick, 'Poets on the Parish', *Times Literary Supplement*, 5091, 27 October 2000: 27.
Share, Don, 'Interviewing', *Essays in Criticism*, 50:4, October 2000: 378-383 [Includes review of the Michael Hamburger interview].

RICHARD WILBUR IN CONVERSATION WITH PETER DALE (2000)

Anon., 'Stand Briefs', *Stand* (New Series), 2:3, September 2000: 133.
Short Notices, *Times Literary Supplement*, 5104, 22 January 2001.

Lancaster, John, *Richard Wilbur News Letter*, 3, Autumn 2001: 7.
Thompson, N.S., 'Typewriter Badminton', *PN Review*, 144, 2002: 90-91.
Unsigned, 'Poetry Comment', *Acumen*, 43, May 2002: 119.

VARIOUS

Atkinson, Christine, 'Our Creative Writers Who Love to Explore Words', *Leighton Buzzard Observer*, 19 December 1989: 10.
Alexander, Michael, 'William Cookson', *The Independent*, 9 January 2003: 16 [Obituary].
Bayley, John, 'Accessibility', *Agenda*, 26:2, Summmer 1988: 38-43 [Peter Dale Issue].
BB., 'William Oxley: Completing the Picture', *Times Literary Supplement*, 4848, 1 March 1996.
Beake, Fred, *Stand*, 37:3, Summer 1996: 77 [*Completing the Picture*, edited by William Oxley].
Beresford, Anne, and Michael Hamburger, 'William Cookson: Dedicated Editor Who Nurtured Poetic Talent', *The Guardian*, 7 January 2003: 18 [Obituary of William Cookson; Details regarding PD inaccurate; See also D.S. below, for 20 September 1996].
Brittan, Simon, 'The Best of *Agenda*', *Times Literary Supplement*, 4773, 23 September 1994: 29.
Brownjohn, Alan, 'A View of English Poetry in the Early Seventies', *British Poetry Since 1960: A Critical Survey*, edited by Michael Schmidt and Grevel Lindop (Carcanet Press, Oxford, 1972): 243-244.
Cookson, William, 'Endnotes', *Agenda*, 26:2, Summmer 1988: 94 [Peter Dale Issue].
Cookson, William, 'Introduction', *Agenda: An Anthology*, *Agenda* (Carcanet, Manchester, 1996): xx-xxi.
Cookson, William, 'The Poetry of Peter Dale', *PNR*, 119, January 1998: 68-69.
Cookson, William, *Agenda*, 38:1-2, Autumn-Winter 2000-2001: 157 [Ronald Duncan Issue].
Crawford, Robert, 'Dear Editors', *Poetry Review*, 1994: 47-48.
Davie, Donald, *Under Briggflats* (Carcanet, Manchester, 1989).
Davis, Dick, 'The Periodicals, 1: *Agenda*', *Times Literary Supplement*, 4193, 12 August 1983.
D. S., 'NB', *Times Literary Supplement*, 4736, 7 January 1994: 12 [*Agenda*].
D. S., 'NB', *Times Literary Supplement*, 4877, 20 September 1996: 16 [Latest issue of *Agenda*].
Editorial Endnote, *Haiku Quarterly*, Spring 1997.
Eagleton, Terry, 'New Poetry', *Stand*, 13:1, 1971-72: 77-79.
Eagleton, Terry, 'The Poetry of Peter Dale', *Agenda*, 13:3, Autumn 1975: 85-91.
Finch, Peter, '*Completing the Picture*: Exiles, Outsiders and Independents', *Poetry Wales*, 31:4, April 1996: 67-69
Finch, Peter, 'A Beginner's Guide', *Writer's Monthly*, November 1991: 12-14.
Fisher, Emma, 'Lit. Mags.', *Spectator*, 6 May 1978: 27.
Forbes, Peter, *Poetry Review*, Autumn/Winter 1996 [Editorial matter concerning the resignation from *Agenda* making use of PD's withdrawal letter to print].
Fraser, G. S., 'Sound before Sense', *Times Literary Supplement*, 3970, 5 May 1978: 496 [*Basil Bunting: Collected Poems*; *Agenda*, Basil Bunting Special Issue'].
Ganz, Robert, 'Vineyard Bookshelf', *Vineyard Gazette* (Martha's Vineyard, Mass.), 31 August 1984 [Rev. of Burnshaw Issue of *Agenda*].
Glover, Michael, 'Just a Smack at Fenton', *New Statesman*, 11 October 1996: 12.
Görtschacher, Wolfgang, *Little Magazine Profiles: The Little Magazines in Great Britain, 1939-1993* (University of Salzburg, Salzburg, 1993): 19, 50, 64, 127-128, 185-186, 212-213, 227, 234, 246, 262, 321, 330-344 (See under Interviews), 406, 479, 527-530, 539, 564-575, 652, 682-684.
Gowrie, Grey, 'Peter Dale', *Agenda*, 13:3, Autumn 1975: 74-84.
Gowrie, Grey, 'Forward For *Agenda*', *Agenda: An Anthology*, *Agenda* (Carcanet, Manchester, 1996): xi.
Gray, Edmund, 'Recollections of Friendship with the Youthful Poundian', *Agenda*, 39:4, Summer 2003: 143-145, 148 [Celebratory Issue for William Cookson].
Haig, Ian, *Agenda*, 9:1, Winter 1971: 37 [Commentary, on 'Wildflower'].
Haems, Catherine, 'Revue des revues étrangères', *Le Courrier*, 196, 1992.
John, Roland, 'Peter Dale: An Appreciation', *Agenda*, 26:2, Summer 1988: 92-93 [Peter Dale Issue].
John, Roland, 'Plotting a Progress: The Poetry of Peter Dale', *Acumen*, 12, October 1990: 36-41.
Lafourcade, Bernard, 'Wyndham Lewis. Du Purgatoire au Panorama', *Études Anglaises*, xxvi:2, 1973: 198.
Levi, Peter, 'Peter Dale', *Agenda*, 26:2, Summmer 1988: 45-46 [Peter Dale Issue].
Lowbury, Edward, 'Verse and Language: Terza Rima in English Poetry', *Hallmarks of Poetry* (University

of Salzburg Studies in English Literature, Salzburg, 1994): 27.
Lucie-Smith, Edward, *British Poetry since 1945* (Penguin, Harmondsworth, 1970): 280 [Headnote].
McCarthy, Patricia, 'Editorial', *Agenda*, 39:4, Summer 2003: 5-6 [Celebratory Issue for William Cookson; See also 'Agenda Broadsheets', *Agenda*, 39.4, Summer 2003: 20].
McCue, Jim, 'Bibliomane', *The Times* (London), 7 June 2003: 41 [Factually inaccurate].
Unsigned [W.S. Milne], 'Obituary, William Cookson', *The Telegraph*, 4 January 2003.
Unsigned [W.S. Milne], 'William Cookson', *The Times*, 8 January 2003: 27 [Obituary].
Nye, Robert, 'Newsy, Intellectual Marines', *The Times*, 28 August 1986.
Oxley, William, 'Peter Dale', *Completing the Picture: Exiles, Outsiders & Independents* (Stride Publications, Exeter, 1995): 58 [Head-note].
Phillpotts, Beatrice, 'Exhibition Marks Limited Edition of Poems and Etchings', *The Advertiser* (Surrey), 15 February 1991.
Powell, Neil, 'Magazine Roundup: No 5: Agenda...', *Poetry Review*, Spring 1993: 72-73.
Rayan, Krishna, *Text and Sub-Text* (Arnold-Heinemann, New Delhi, 1987): 73.
Selbourne, Anthony, 'Poetry Flourishes in Surrey', *Surrey Advertiser*, 20 July 1990.
Shepherd, Michael, 'Guts, the Romantic and the Religious', *Art News and Review*, 1959 [Review of art exhibition, *Visceral Image* (including framed holographs of poems by PD), The Woodstock Gallery, London].
Stanford, Derek, Book Reviews, The Weekend Review, *The Statesman*, 1984.
Taylor, Robert, 'Bookmaking', *Boston Sunday Globe*, 23 September 1984.
Thompson, N. P., *The Dark Horse*, 15, Summer 2003 [Interview of Philip Hoy concerning Between the Lines Press].
Tunnicliffe, Stephen, *Poetry Experience: Teaching and Writing Poetry in Secondary Schools* (Methuen, London/New York, 1984): 48, 85, 90, 92.
Unsigned, *Times Educational Supplement*, 4 January 1983 [Magazine round-up].
Unsigned, 'School Pupils See Poetry in Real Motion', *Guardian* (Sutton), 22 July 1982: 5 [Includes group photograph].
Unsigned, 'Stanley Burnshaw: "The Poet Himself"', *Vineyard Gazette* (Martha's Vineyard, Mass.), 23 August 1984.
Wade, Stephen, 'Englishness and Estrangement in the Poetry of Michael Hamburger', *Agenda*, 35:3, Autumn 1997: 76 [Hamburger Issue].
Williams, Hugo, 'Freelance', *Times Literary Supplement*, 4947, 23 January 1998: 16.
Wright, David, 'Another Part of the Wood', *Poetry Nation*, 4, 1975: 121.
Zaller, Robert, *Elegies: The Tribute of His Peers for Robinson Jeffers* (Tor House Press, Carmel, California, 1989): xxxii.

REVIEWS OF PLAYS

Gurney, John, 'The Image of the Woman in Peter Dale's *Cell* and *Sephe*', *Agenda*, 26:2, Summer 1988: 89-91 [Peter Dale Issue].
Wade, Stephen, 'Peter Dale's *Cell*: Allegory and Personal Autonomy', *Agenda*, 18:4-19:1, Winter-Spring 1981: 129-134].

REVIEWS OF TRANSLATIONS

THE LEGACY AND OTHER POEMS OF FRANÇOIS VILLON (1971)

Anon. [Dunn, Douglas], 'Back to Modernism', *Times Literary Supplement*, 3684, 13 October 1972: 1217.
Nye, Robert, 'The Age of Translation', *The Times*, 30 December 1971.
Maclean, A. D., 'The Legacy', *Times Literary Supplement*, 3688, 10 November 1972 [Letter].

THE LEGACY, THE TESTAMENT, AND OTHER POEMS OF FRANÇOIS VILLON (1973)

Anon. [Eagleton, Terry], 'Inroads into the Past', *Times Literary Supplement*, 3735, 5 October 1973:

1154.
Anon., Choice, July/August 1974: 767.
Bonnerot, Louis, 'Peter Dale's Villon', Agenda, 11:4-12:1, Autumn-Winter 1973-74: 122-138.
Johnson, Anthony L., 'Reviews', Littack, 1980: 10.
Levin, Bernard, 'The Great Untranslatable', Observer, 25 November 1973.
Nye, Robert, 'Poetry', The Times, 24 October 1973.
Osburn, C. B., Library Journal, 1 December 1973: 3565.
Raine, Craig, 'The Rivals', Times Educational Supplement, 3 May 1974.
Wall, Alan, 'In a Month of Sundays', London Review of Books, 25 May 1995 [Letter to the editor].

THE SEASONS OF CANKAM (1975)

Hamilton, Robin, Aquarius, 9, 1977: 72.
Wade, Stephen, Littack, 10, November 1975: 64.

SELECTED POEMS OF FRANÇOIS VILLON (1978; 1988; 1994)

Burl, Aubrey, Danse Macabre: Francois Villon, Poetry, & Murder in Medieval France (Sutton Publishing, Stroud, Gloucestershire, 2000): vi, 63, 88, 159, 216 [Various references, quotations].
Clarke, David, 'Les Pendus de Montfaucon, 1493', A Late Flowering (Hippopotamus Press, Frome, Somerset, 1993): 49 [Poem; A curiosity which deals with cover of Penguin Edition of PD's Villon but does not identify the translator].
Cooke, David, 'The Fascination of What's Difficult: Peter Dale's Translations of Villon and Laforgue', Dale Issue, Agenda, 26:2, Summer 1988: 74-87.
Davie, Donald, 'Peter Dale's Villon', Agenda, 26:2, Summer 1988: 65-73 [Peter Dale Issue].
Hofstadter, Douglas R., Le Ton Beau de Marot: In Praise of The Music of Language (Bloomsbury/Basic Books, London/New York, 1997): 222-224, 557.
Howard, Philip, 'Fair Sweet Friends', The Times, 23 June 1978.
Levin, Bernard, 'Pain, No Matter How You Write It', The Times Saturday Review, 2 November 1991: 38.

NARROW STRAITS: POEMS FROM THE FRENCH (1985)

Crouch, Marcus, 'Literature: Poetry', The School Librarian, 1986: 193.
Hendriks, A. L., 'A Note on Narrow Straits', Outposts, 156, Spring 1988: 76-77.
Oxley, William, 'Narrow Straits', Core, June 1987.
Pugh, Sheenagh, Poetry Wales, 22:1: 93-95.
Pursglove, Glyn, Acumen, 5, April 1987: 97-99.
Romer, Stephen, 'In Different Voices', Times Literary Supplement, 4383, 3 April 1987: 364.
Stanford, Derek, 'Peter Dale, Narrow Straits', Agenda, 24:1, Spring 1986: 39.
Sail, Lawrence, Stand, 28:3, Summer 1987: 75.
Suter, Anthony, Outposts, 156, Spring 1988: 68-75.
Wade, Stephen, Proof (Lincoln), December 1986.

POEMS OF JULES LAFORGUE (1986; 2001)

Attal, Jean-Paul, 'Poésie et Traduction', La Tribune Internationale des Langues Vivantes, 32, November 2002: 60-61 [Cover numbered 31, Mai 2002, on contents page].
Enright, D. J., 'Bilingual Pleasures', Observer, 16 March 1986.
Enright, D. J., 'Books of the Year', Observer, 30 November 1986.
Glover, Michael, 'French Literature', British Book News, August 1986.
Holmes, Anne, 'Laforgue: Poems of Jules Laforgue', French Studies, 44, pt 1, 1988.
Levi, Peter, 'Peter Dale's Laforgue', Agenda, 24:3, Autumn 1986: 89-92 [Peter Levi Issue].

Milne, William S., *PNR*, 57, Spring 1986: 4 [Letter to the editors regarding PD's Laforgue translation].
Nelson, Graham, 'French Poetry', *Thumbscrew*, 20-21, 2002: 143-145.
Pursglove, Glyn, 'Poetry Comment', *Acumen*, 41, September 2001: 114-115.
Romer, Stephen, 'In Different Voices', *Times Literary Supplement*, 4383, 3 April 1987: 364.
Sorrell, Martin, 'Three English Versions of Jules Laforgue's "Pierrots" no. 1' [from *L'Imitation de Notre-Dame la lune*], *Journal of European Studies*, xxiv, 1994: 369-384.

The Divine Comedy (1996; 1998; 2001; 2003; 2004)

Attal, Jean-Paul, 'Poésie et Traduction', *La Tribune Internationale des Langues Vivantes*, 32, November 2002: 60-61 [Cover numbered 31, Mai 2002, on contents page].
Bold, Alan, 'A Head of His Time', *The Herald* (Glasgow), 28 December 1996: 12.
Cooksey, T. L., 'Dante: The Divine Comedy', *Library Journal*, 19 January 1997.
Ellis, Steve, 'Terza Rima Tightrope', *Poetry Review*, 87:2, Summer 1997: 55.
The Divine Comedy (Guernica Publishers, Canada, September-December, March 1996) [Publisher's catalogue announcement].
John, Roland, 'The Importance of Dante', *Acumen*, 31, May 1998: 63-65.
John, Roland, '*The Divine Comedy* translated by Peter Dale', *Outposts*, 184, Autumn 1998: 107.
Knottenbelt, E.M., 'Translating Dante', *Times Literary Supplement*, 5055, 18 February 2000: 17 [Letter to the editor].
Meyer, Ole, 'Dante's *Divine Comedy*: Epic or Novel?', *ITI Colloquium on Literary Translation* (University of Sheffield, 2 September 1998) [Workshop].
Milne, W. S., 'Laurence Binyon', *Agenda*, 39:1-3, Winter 2002-03: 380-382.
Thompson, N. S., 'From Horror to Awe', *Times Literary Supplement*, 4938, 21 November 1997: 26.
Unsigned, Dante review, *Translation Review*, January 1998.
Unsigned, 'Forecasts', *Publishers' Weekly*, 26 May 1997.
Unsigned, *Journal of the Academy of American Poets*, Summer 1997 [Round-up].
Wheatley, David, 'Rhyming His Way Between Heaven and Hell', *The Irish Times*, 29 January 1997: 16.

Poems of François Villon: The Legacy, The Testament & Other Poems (2001)

Attal, Jean-Paul, 'Poésie et Traduction', *La Tribune Internationale des Langues Vivantes*, 32, November 2002: 60-61 [Cover numbered 31, Mai 2002, on contents page].
Falck, Colin, *American and British Verse in the Twentieth Century: The Poetry that Matters* (Ashgate, Aldershot, Hants, England/Burlington, Vermont, 2003): xii, 226, 244n, 245.
Nelson, Graham, 'French Poetry', *Thumbscrew*, 20-21, 2002: 143-145.
Pursglove, Glyn, 'Poetry Comment', *Acumen*, 41, September 2001: 114-115.
Scannell, Vernon, 'Poète Maudit and Poems of Illness', *Sunday Telegraph*, 29 July 2001.

Various

Daems, Catherine, 'Revue des revues étrangères', *Le Courrier* (Brussels), 196, 1992.
Davie, Donald, *Under Briggflatts: A History of Poetry in Great Britain, 1960-88* (Carcanet, Manchester, 1989) [Remarks].
Passannanti, Erminia, 'Gesto' ('Gesture'), 'Tacito' ('Unspoken'), 'Il Sentiero infossato' ('The Sunken Path'), *Immaginazione*, January-February 1998: 4-6 [Article in Italian accompanying her translations].

Listings in Reference Works

Contemporary Literary Criticism, edited by Carolyn Riley and Barbara Harte (Gale Research Company, Detroit, 1974): 58-59 [Extract by PD on Berryman].
Cookson, William, 'Dale, Peter', *Contemporary Poets of the English Language* (St James Press, London, 1970): 260-261.
Contemporary Poets, edited by James Vinson and D.L. Kirkpatrick (St Martins Press, New York, 1985).

Hyland, Paul, *Getting into Poetry: A Readers' & Writers' Guide to the Poetry Scene* (Newcastle upon Tyne, Bloodaxe Books, 1992): 86-88.
International Who's Who in Poetry, 5th Edition, Ernest Kay (International Biographical Centre, Cambridge UK, 1976) [See also previous and numerous other editions].
International Who's Who in Poetry 2005 (Europa Publications, 2005).
People of Surrey, edited by Juliet Hine (Debrett's Peerage Limited, London, 1991): 40.
Poetry Live – British and Irish Poetry 1987, edited by John Medlin (Book Trust/Poetry Society, London, 1987): 7.
Prunty, Wyatt, *Dictionary of Literary Biography* (Gale, Detroit, 1986): 86-93.
Pursglove, Glyn, 'Dale, Peter (John)', *Contemporary Poets*, 5th Edition (St James Press, Detroit, 1995).
Seymour-Smith, Martin, *The Oxford Companion to Twentieth Century Poetry*, edited by Ian Hamilton (Oxford University Press, Oxford, 1994): 114.
The Oxford Companion to Twentieth Century Literature, edited by Jenny Stringer (Oxford University Press, Oxford/New York, 1996): 154.
Who's Who in Poetry, 9th edition (International Biographical Centre, Cambridge, 1999).
Who's Who in the World, vol. 3 (Marquise Who's Who Inc., Chicago, 1976).
Who's Who of Authors and Writers, 2005 (Europa Publications, 2005).
Writers' Directory (St James Press, Farmington Hills, Michigan, 1999).
Contemporary Poets, edited by Thomas Riggs (St James Press, Farmington, Michigan, 2000) [Includes updated statement by PD].
International Authors and Writers Who's Who (Biographical Centre, Cambridge, 2001) [Seventeenth and previous editions].

BIOGRAPHICAL

Unsigned, 'Story of the Battlefield', *Peace News*, 28 August 1958.
Unsigned, 'Addlestone's Modern Poet', *The Review* (Woking), July 1966.
Unsigned, 'Familiar Scenes in Poet's New Volume', *The Surrey Herald*, 26 January 1968.
Lovelock, Yann, 'Blue Jeans and Gown: The Beat Scene in Oxford, 1959-62', *The Road to Parnassus: Peter Russell on His Seventieth Birthday* (University of Salzburg Press, Salzburg, 1996): 477-491.
Unsigned, 'Cyclist's Delight', *Sutton Advertiser*, 10 February 1983 [With photograph and garbled article].
'Peter Dale', *The Churchill Clarion* (Woking, Surrey), July 1994 [Headnote with photograph].
Oxley, William, *No Accounting for Paradise* (Rockingham Press, Ware, Herts., 1999): 197-198.
McCarthy, Patricia, *Agenda*, 37:4, Spring-Summer 2000: 6 [Editorial quoting William Cookson].
Jacobson, Dan, *Ian Hamilton in Conversation with Dan Jacobson* (Between the Lines, London, 2002): 35, 42, 45.

MUSICAL SETTINGS

Clarke, Nigel, *The Market Place* [Musical Play for Primary Schools; First performed at opening of the John Davis Music and Arts Centre, St Edward's C. E. Primary School, Romford, Essex, 10 October 1984].
Clarke, Nigel, *In the Dark Time: A Carol* [First performed by Surbiton Oratorio Society, Christmas Concert, 15th December 1984].
Clucas, Humphrey, *In The Dark Time: Carol for Upper Voices and Organ or Piano* (Animus, Dalton in Furness, Spring 1998) [by Uppingham School choir in Peterborough Cathedral, Christmas 1999; Revised, shorter text of previous carol].
Le Fleming, Anthony, *In the Dark Time* (Ana Publishing Limited, Southsea, 2004) [New setting of text; First performed in Holy Trinity Church, Clapham, 2003].

REVIEWS OF MUSICAL SETTINGS

Edwards, Michael, 'Choral Music by Anthony le Fleming', *The Organists' Review*, February 2004: 82-

84.
Wickham, Edward, 'How to Avoid a Soap-and-Tie Carol Service', *The Church Times*, 8 October 1999: 32 [Rev. of Clucas's setting for 'In the Dark Time'].

RECORDINGS OF MUSICAL SETTINGS

'In the Dark Time', (sound disc, 2000) [Clucas setting; Performed by Uppingham School choir in Peterborough Cathedral, Christmas 1999].

AUDIO-RECORDINGS OF POEMS

Poetry Reading: Tape 2109, British Council – Recorded Sound Section, dubbed 31, January 1977, 22 minutes 10 seconds: poems: 'Dedication to P.'; 'The Visitors'; 'Courtesy Visit'; 'The Terms'; 'Thinking of Writing a Letter'; 'Starting your Travels'; 'The Swifts'; 'Returns'; 'Gift of Words'; 'Twilight'; 'Keepsake'; 'The Mind's Eye'; 'Crowd'; 'Old Poet on a Rainy Day'; 'The Rose'; 'Shades'; 'One Another'; 'Walk'; 'Fledgling'; 'Spectrum'; 'Dusk'. [PD had bronchitis at the time of this reading and the voice is husky unintentionally.]
The Poet Speaks: Peter Dale interviewed by Peter Orr: Tape 2110, British Council, Recorded Sound Section, dubbed 31 January 1977, 27 minutes 45 seconds. [See end of previous entry.] [These are also in the Harvard University Library of Modern Poetry.]
One Another, seventeen sonnets from it, at the launch of the Waywiser Edition, audio recording of the Voicebox reading, Southbank Centre, 2 May 2002.

EXHIBITION INCLUSIONS

Visceral Image Exhibition (The Woodstock Gallery, New Bond Street, London, 1959) [With draughtsman/painter Michael Foley, painter Eddie Wolfram, and sculptor, Isaac Witkin, taped jazz by Peter Buss, and including framed holographs of poems by PD].
Making Waves: *Six Twentieth Century Poets*: with etchings by John Tatchell Freeman, and drawings by Penelli: The Poetry Library, Royal Festival Hall, London, January – 1 February 1991; The Hawth, Crawley, Sussex, 27 April – 11 May 1991; The Charterhouse Festival, 12 September 1991.
Making Waves: International Poetry and Graphics Exhibition, including nineteenth-century translations of French verse by P.D. with accompanying etchings by John Tatchell Freeman: ('To a Woman Passing', Baudelaire; 'Plaint', Charles Cros; 'Morning', Charles Cros; 'Complaint of Consolations', Laforgue; 'Ballade about Returning', Laforgue; 'Paris by Night', Corbière.) South Hill Park Centre, Bracknell, 4 June–25 June 1993; Strang Print Room Foyer, University College, London, from 31 October 1994. [And elsewhere.]

PORTRAITS

Bevan, J., 'Untitled' [Ink Sketch; PD personal collection].
'P.D. by P.E.', circa 1975 [Two ink cartoons measuring 10cm x 20.5cm; initialed by P.E.; PD personal collection].
Andrews, Bernard, 'Peter Dale', *Agenda*, 26:2, Summer 1988 [Dry-point; Peter Dale Issue].
Andrews, Bernard, 'Peter Dale in his Study', *Agenda*, 26:2, Summer 1988 [Ink sketch; Peter Dale Issue].
Wolfram, Eddie, 'Peter Dale', 1992 [Ink sketch; One of a series of poets' portraits made for The Sixties Issue of *Agenda* but not used; PD personal collection].
Wolfram, Eddie, 'The Young Peter Dale', 1994 [Acrylic on canvas measuring two foot by four; PD personal collection].
Coleman, Mike, 'Portrait of Peter Dale II', 1998 [Acrylic on paper measuring 59cm x 84cm; Coleman personal collection; Published in *The BritArt Directory* (Sheffield, 2001): 60].
Coleman, Mike, 'Peter Dale', 1998 [Acrylic on paper measuring 59cm x 84cm; Coleman personal collection].

The Dale Archives

The Bodleian Library, Oxford

A holograph notebook of *One Another* [Shelf-mark MS Eng. e. 2401].

St Peter's College Library Archives, Oxford

A holograph notebook of the second edition of *One Another*, source text of *Edge to Edge* revision.
A bibliography from 1958-1999.

Harry Ransom Humanities Research Center, University of Texas, Austin, USA

Copies of letters to Stanley Burnshaw.

The Beinecke Library, Yale

Agenda association material in the *Agenda* archives.

The Brotherton Library, Leeds University

Between the Lines material relating to interviews with Hamburger, Thwaite, Donald Hall, Richard Wilbur, PD, etc.
An Essay on Villon, corrected notebook.
Da Capo, papers, etc., including Philip Hoy's.
Earth Light, holograph, corrected notebook, corrected hardback.
The Dark Voyage, holograph, corrected notebook; *Agenda* text, overwritten; typescript with corrections.
Too Much of Water, holograph, corrected notebook, corrected hardback.
Under the Breath, notebook, proofs, corrected typescript, letters and notes.

THE CRITICS

WALK FROM THE HOUSE (1962)

'The emotion here is in the way things happen, in a sort of lyric drama best illustrated by "Unaddressed Letter" ...' – Wallace Kaufman, *Isis*, 23 January 1963

'There is more than embryonic talent here; it is genuine poetry in the making.' – Anon., 'Pathway to Parnassus', *Times Literary Supplement*, 26 July 1963

'... Peter Dale ... strikes me as being rather muddled, as though the emotional lines of his verse were more obscured by his words than revealed by them.' – A. Alvarez, 'New Poetry in Paperback', Weekend Review, *The Observer*, 13 January 1963

'The positive qualities that Dale shows himself to possess in such poems are: an ability to fix experiences permanently in words that are unalterably part of them...' – William Cookson, review of four Fantasy Press Poets, *Agenda* 2.11-12, March-April 1963

'His method is a kind of insistent descriptive mastery of the situation. ... Dale settles for his style too easily... But there is a kind of honesty in this which is better than any amount of crankiness.' – Colin Falck, 'The Lyrical Man', *The Review* 5, 1963

THE STORMS (1968)

'Mr Dale's tough-tender mood becomes trying as poem after poem is spoken warily out of the corner of the mouth.' – Anon., 'Verse and Versatility', *Times Literary Supplement*, 15 February 1968

'[The poems in *The Storms*] will get themselves read willy nilly, in the end.' – Bill Byrom, America: 'English Groundswell in the East', The Saturday Review, *The Times*, 4 May 1968

'... [H]is first book is a disappointment. The poems are sentimental and, though self-conscious, un-self-aware.' – Martin Dodsworth, *The Listener*, 1 February 1968

'But to be clear is not to be simple. Every reading of *The Storms* brings something fresh, and reveals new elements of complexity – for there is notable multiplicity both of viewpoint and in the use of different kinds of language.' – Edmund Gray, 'Peter Dale and the Imagination', *Agenda* 6.2, Spring 1968, 75-80

'There are some moving moments and an impressively minute kind of observation is at work throughout but there is a flat, inert quality in many of the poems, a sterile hopelessness.' – Ian Hamilton, 'Bringing Out the Worst', *The Observer*, 11 February 1968

'Why have we not heard more of Peter Dale's *The Storms*? His first book is a strong and subtle one.' – X. J. Kennedy, 'The Devalued Estate', *Poetry* (Chicago), July 1969

'The subsuming principle for all Dale's poetry is relationship. Because of his preoccupation with relationships, rather than the isolated self that dominates much contemporary writing, Dale's is a particularly civilized and constructive poetry. The subjective turns that do occur in his poems always include another person, indeed take much of their meaning from that other person.' – Wyatt Prunty in *Contemporary Poets*, 1983

'At his best, as in "Single Ticket" ... Dale is awkward, ingenuous and interesting in a Hardyesque way.' – Julian Symons, 'MacSpaunday', *New Statesman*, 1 March 1968

MORTAL FIRE (1970)

'His expertise in death and renewal (documented by a set of poems on hospital service) can lift his plain style to the level of moving art.' – Irvin Ehrenpreis, 'Moments of Suffocation', *Times Literary Supplement*, 2 July 1970

'Dale has found the knack of preserving that emotional economy while simultaneously developing and expanding it into a complete poetic statement. This happens most evidently in two excellent poems, "Unaddressed Letter", and "The Fragments" ...' – Terry Eagleton, 'New Poetry', *Stand* 11, 1970

'Much English post-war poetry could be described perhaps unkindly as "suburban sensational"; if Peter Dale's appears in this class, it is the best of the genre after Larkin.' – David Jay, 'Suburban Sensation', *Times Educational Supplement*, 18 September 1970

'Dale is always tactful with language, his elegiac note is varied and his cadences sound well. I just wish he would move from the confessional shadow into a more active world. ... But the best writing in *Mortal Fire* is so skilful, it would be good to see him attempting larger things.' – Peter Porter, 'In the Bosom of the Family', *London Magazine*, September 1970, 70

'In single poems – "Unaddressed Letter" and in one or two sections of the "Having No Alternative" sequence – a more stirring energetic note is heard and the love poems that are printed near the end of the book are a good deal more energetic and incisive than anything Dale has done before – not least because they are free of the fiddling rhyme-schemes he has so often toyed with in the past.' – Ian Hamilton, 'A Matter of Balance', *Observer*, 19 July 1970

'Dale's best poems seem the work of another writer, but even in them the diction isn't free from uncertainties.' – Stephen Wall, 'Letting it Happen', *The Review* 23, September -November 1970

Mortal Fire (1976)

'In *Mortal Fire*, the generosity and sensitivity towards experience, which seem to me the finest features of this poet, work with increasing metaphoric intensity, bringing to ordinary experience the illumination and value of the poetic.' – William Bedford, 'Fathers and Sons: Peter Dale's *Mortal Fire*', *The Southern Review*, Winter 1979

'Inside each of the remnants thus sewn together, the needlework is often very fine and intricate indeed. That, too, was what one meant by "strangulated": a voice so devoted to nuance, how could it ever speak out? It took a wrong way out – everyone seems to agree – in the verse-drama "Cell".

This other way it has taken – of orchestrating into a full tone its own sotto voce utterances – though it creates some obscurities and a certain harshness in driving together tones that belong apart, has nevertheless arrived, on balance, at an audacious, costly achievement which puts Peter Dale out in front of those anti-rhetorical rhetoricians with whom he seemed to be running in concert a couple of years ago.' – Donald Davie, 'Father's Story', *The Listener*, 28 October 1976

'What is evident throughout the book in both the successful and a number of the failures, is Mr Dale's gift for striking remarkable visual images.' – John Mole, 'Man Is a Landscape', *Times Literary Supplement*, 1 October 1976

'Dale is one of the subtlest rimers in English since Emily Dickinson: like her he is dextrous in his use of off-rimes ...' – Jan Schreiber, 'Peter Dale's *Mortal Fire*', *Canto* 1.1, Andover, Mass., Spring 1977

One Another (1978)

'But where *Modern Love* was dramatic, *One Another* takes, as its title implies, a synthesis of shared experience, and makes it extraordinarily vivid and accessible to the ordinary unengaged reader.' – John Bayley, 'Accessibility', *Agenda* 26.2, Summer 1988

'In some of the early poems, for instance, linguistic reticence sometimes involved a sacrifice of poetic intensity to narrative structure ... *One Another* is a largely successful reconciliation of these tensions, and for the first time, Dale has produced a substantial work in which the fusion of narrative line and poetic intensity is complete. The problem of course is that although his achievement is essentially part of his method, the result is an extremely complex and sometimes confusing narrative.' – William Bedford, 'Narrative and Epiphany', *Agenda* 17.1, Spring 1979

Peter Dale's new collection seems to me certainly the most distinguished he has produced to date. ... This use of natural imagery is a relatively fresh departure for Dale, a poet of streets, rooms, hospitals; and the diplomacy with which it is deployed is all the more striking.' – Terry Eagleton, 'New Poetry', *Stand* 20.1, 1978-9

'"One Another" grasps the interfusion that takes place between two people who have been together for years. While Frost's "Spring Pools" represents a naturalistic interfusion, Dale's is anthropomorphic without apology. ... "One Another" insists on going a step farther than Frost's poem, and it is the better poem for doing so.' – Wyatt Prunty, 'Reciprocals', *The Southern Review*, USA, July 1981

'... [The sonnets] make great use of the sense of touch – the word itself occurs widely and is well used to evoke the meeting-point, and the limit of meeting, between two personalities. Other contiguous opposites, notably light and darkness (with their gradations of brightness and shadow), are deployed to build up and vary the closeness of the relationship, giving the sonnets a kind of cumulative power which is skilfully worked for. The lyrical tone strikingly evokes the Hardy of 1912-13 – autumnal, a world of wet leaves and a haunted heart ... But Dale is more sensuous than Hardy – Hardy under the influence of Baudelaire, almost, hair being another favourite image here. Good though some of the individual sonnets are his sequence does not wholly live up to the claims which the author makes for it.' – Lawrence Sail, 'Working the Middle Ground', *Poetry Review* 69.2, 1979

'It is poetry of a very high order, quite worthy to be mentioned in the same breath as that published in its decade by Philip Larkin, Geoffrey Hill and F.T. Prince.... I can't point out the bright essence of the book – it's everywhere, but nowhere on the page specifically.' – W. G. Shepherd, 'Solipsism Transcended', Seventies Issue, *Agenda* 33.1, January 1995

'The impression this book leaves, then, is of a fine sensibility adrift in a beautiful mist which never quite cleared.' – Anne Stevenson, 'Being happy', *The Listener*, 15 March 1979

'Nor does the poet ever succeed in assuming the woman's voice and persona, as he attempts to do in many sonnets.
　　Nevertheless, *One Another* is an impressive and moving sequence; courageous also – again – in touching so truthfully the intimacies we find unspeakable ...' – D. M. Thomas, 'The Habits of Love', *Times Literary Supplement*, October 1978

'[The sonnets'] craftsmanship, closely united with their intellectual-emotional content both ensure a poetry that goes beyond verbal dexterity and present poetic fantasy. Akin to the poetry of Jon Stallworthy, Ian Hamilton, even to that of Philip Larkin, Peter Dale's sonnets are in that community, as were his earlier poems of *Mortal Fire*.' – Anne Tibble, *Outposts* 123, Winter 1979

One Another (2002)

'He is quite capable of complex moral and ethical reasoning in verse, as readers of his early *Mortal Fire* will know. The construction of these poems on a quite different principle is thus evidently a conscious choice – one that asks a different mind set of the reader ...' – Jan Schreiber, 2004

'The best of these poems are engaging, immediate and direct – to the point where the writer disappears and the reader is confronted intimately with the subject – as if thought and feeling, and observation, derive exclusively from within the reader's mind, perception and reacaction seamlessly one.' – David Storey, 2002

Too Much of Water (1983)

'It is in the lyrical sweetness and bitterness of his poems ... that Peter Dale still impresses one ... Dale has continued to develop his skills into capturing a whole range of commonplace events with the same characteristically bitter-sweet music.' – David Annwn, *Labrys*, 10 May 1984

'This seriousness ... has enabled him to write some of our more moving poems of the last fifteen years....
 The poet's passion is solely for his craft, it is not to be found within the language of the poem. This coolness keeps Dale truthful and capable of making the poems an emotionally and artistically convincing whole.' – Jonathan Barker, 'Attendant Shadows', *PNR*, Autumn 1984

'I mention these points at such length because they seem to me to illustrate something characteristic of the method and themes of *Too Much of Water*. Individual poems offer a view which is immediately countered by an alternative, and out of the conflict some sort of resolution is eventually worked. Much of the material is arranged as an argument, usually between a man and a woman, often between imagination and "realism" ...
 This is poetry doing what it should always do. Exploring the language, charging it with meaning, telling us something about being alive. I've always admired Peter Dale's work, and *Too Much of Water* is a considerable addition to his constantly developing talent.' – William Bedford, '"Redolence returning, touched with brine"', *Agenda* 22.3-4, Autumn-Winter 1984-5

'Sometimes wistful, often pessimistic, invariably interesting, his work is not to be lightly dismissed.' – Martin Haslehurst, review, *Anglo-Welsh Review* 76, 1984

'His emphasis on will means that he tries to go without the pleasures for which we often read, the things and scenes remembered and treasured out of context: "Last Wishes" shows how much he could achieve in that direction if he would only let "feeling's fluke" have its head.' – Lachlan Mackinnon, 'Preening and glazing', *Times Literary Supplement*, 27 July 1984
 ... [T]here is what is almost everywhere in this collection: an almost Lucretian sense of mutability and transient human attachment mixed with a tone close to that of Hardy's best love poems to Emma: then, a fastidious and self-disciplined feel to the diction in

almost every poem.

There are certain poems in this collection – "Last Wishes", "Spring", "Interflora", and "Rendezvous" especially, where the fusion of these elements creates wonderfully successful poetry to match Heaney's "Mid-Term Break", and the best of his evocative poems on Derry. ...

The force and imagery he employs will always lift the most plain setting or subject into another area of feeling. This is a rich and impressive book which goes beyond much of his earlier lyrics, yet retains the skill with "making" poetry that has been evident in the translations.' – Stephen Wade, 'Too Much of Water', *Agenda* 22.3-4, Autumn-Winter 1984-85

Earth Light (1991)

'*Mirrors, Windows* does seem an extraordinarily controlled poem, an elegiac, beautiful and in the best sense consoling reflection on the difficulties of human relations, of love and families, of memory and endurance.' – William Bedford, 'Earth Light, Peter Dale', *Agenda* 29.4, Winter 1991

'What is "strange" about all this is Dale's unrelenting seriousness and his devotion to a small, clearly defined group of concerns. This in turn tells us much about what we have been led to expect from poetry but it also reminds us that all kinds of poetry continue to be written outside the currents of fashion and the achievements of each generation's "star players". I can't say I find much to enjoy in Dale's downbeat wistful imagism but there is real craft here and his work always evokes a response. whether one finds neglected virtues or a redundant fogeyism makes a useful litmus test.' – David Kennedy, 'Beyond Local Borders', *PNR* 19.3, January-February 1993

'"Like a Vow" ... tackles one of the main, perennial tasks of poetry – the definition of emotion.... My problem in wishing to describe the resultant work is the undesirabilty, even impossibility, of distinguishing the emotion from the definition, the response in my mind to the poem itself. Poem and response are specific and real, but not reducible to the ratiocinative terms of critical prose. Also, what we have here is not a definition of past, finished emotion (c.f. "emotion recollected in tranquillity"), but a dynamic open-ended striving to discover and embrace emotional realities which are very present, are in the poem's "now". and this quality of searching, the difficulty of finding, is itself part of the emotion-to-be-defned.' – W. G. Shepherd, 'Earth Light', *Outposts* 171, Winter 1991

'But the precise versification, the tercets, the persuasive off-rhymes, keep everything firmly under control, and mostly at tantalising arms' [sic] length ... Like many of the poems this conceals rather than becomes revealing, and that is entirely Peter Dale's business; but the poetry is entirely mine, [sic] and I regret the customary coolness of its temperature.' – Eddie Wainwright, 'Alpha to Omega', *Envoi*, 1992

'The curt monosyllables [of "Occasions"] straining against the sentiment of a deeply felt love poem, the precise yet suggestive evocations of a long, shared life, the enigma of the third stanza turned sharply by the unexpected desolation of the fourth – here is poetry as finely wrought and fiercely compact as three decades of experience and craft can make it. Yet this is only one of Dale's voices, and he is willing to give his line play, turn colloquial, or even risk the flat uninflected tone of a John Ashbery as to practice the tautness and control that compels one's most immediate admiration.' – Robert Zaller, *The Texas Review* 14.1-2, Summer 1993

EDGE TO EDGE: NEW AND SELECTED POEMS (1996)

'*Edge to Edge* can be absorbing, and is a monument to this poet's unfashionable kind of integrity.' – Alan Brownjohn, 'The Mark of the Mature', Books, *The Sunday Times*, 26 January 1997

'Peter Dale has wrongly been termed a pastoral poet. Although his poems have "the colour of nature" his theme is really the mystery of human consciousness. This becomes particularly clear in the next major sequence, "Like a Vow", a poem of memory, place and the power of landscape on the mind. It develops from themes in *One Another*, "Eyes, eyes, that bear in mind this meagre land / look back – hold me stronger than the place" ...' – William Cookson, 'The Poetry of Peter Dale', *PNR* 119, 1998

'Larkin, who really was a master of colloquial phrases, would never have misused them as Dale does here. It would of course be unfair to condemn the book because of such flaws. They do, however, indicate what I distrust about Dale's enterprise: the determination to be both plain-speaking and at the same time sensitive comes across as not so much a triumph of poetic personality (in the Yeatsian sense) but as an act of will.' – John Lucas, *Stand* 39.2, Spring 1998

'But accessibility in a poem is not a fault, but a way into the poem. It should mean, and with Dale it certainly does, that the poem works not only on one level but on several and, once attracted by its comprehensibility, it is possible to read time and time again and go on finding new discoveries.

Peter Dale's poetry is in the great line of English poetry. He is not a copy of the great romantics, nor the Victorian tradition, and less so of the Georgian, because he is a unique voice but the influences are there.' – Ted Griffiths, '*Edge to Edge: New and Selected Poems*', *Outposts* 184, Autumn 1998

'The highest praise one can bestow on a poet, it seems to me, is to suggest that at certain times he or she catches the truth for us all. Such a poem is "A Time to Speak".' – Michael Kilby, 'The Poetry of Peter Dale', *Agenda* 35.1, 1997

'One can applaud Peter Dale's technique for its own sake, without necessarily liking the style – in this case rather stilted and with little tonal modulation. The note constantly sounded – mortality – inevitably grows wearisome, though it's interesting to note that obsession is precisely what the writer urges his son to cultivate in "Wise and Cautious", a moving and depressing poem.' – Eva Salzman, 'The Formal and the fast-food', *TLS*, 3 July 1992

'Dale's work needs no recommendation. It is there as a body of writing at the centre of the art.' – Stephen Wade, *Acumen* 33, January 1998

D*A* C*APO* (1997)

'The sequence is of characteristic subtlety and emotional weight – as much in what is left unuttered as in what is made explicit ... Not for the first time, Dale has produced, in relatively few pages, an implied narrative with the range and suggestiveness of most novels many times its length.' – Glyn Pursglove,'Poetry Comment', *Acumen* 31, May 1998

Dale deserves to be ranked as one of the great poets of relationships, a worthy heir to Tennyson, Meredith, Patmore, Browning, Clough, Hardy, Graves, Frost. – Philip Hoy, 'Proem' to *Da Capo*, Agenda Editions/Poets and Painters Press, 1997

U*NDER THE* B*REATH* (2002)

'Some "Tirades" ... take up myth or narrative and become more lyrical. But the poems are generally tight-lipped, passionately ironic, yet paradoxically tender dialogues, depending more on statement than imagery; and they're probably necessarily, securely knotted in rhyme or pararhyme.' – Herbert Lomas, 'Sliding Carpets', *The London Magazine*, June-July 2003

'Michael Kelly, reviewing *Edge to Edge*, wrote: "The highest praise one can bestow on a poet, it seems to me, is to suggest that at certain times he or she catches the truth for us all." It seems to me that "Half-light" is another poem of this quality and that there are many poems of that quality in this volume.' – W. S. Milne, 'Insidious Mastery', *Acumen* 46, May 2003

'The first three poems in this collection "Answer", "Visitation" and "Nocturne" are breathtaking. The unguarded intensity of feeling is transformed by a precision of voice expressing this feeling that has created three truly great elegies.' – Judy Gahagan, 'Peter Dale: Under the Breath', *Ambit* 175, January 2004

TRANSLATIONS

P*OEMS OF* J*ULES* L*AFORGUE* (1986)

'It isn't merely that Dale's feet fit neatly into Laforgue's shoes, for he contrives to replace a French skin with an English one ... The collection is hard to over-praise. – D. J. Enright, 'Bilingual pleasures', *Observer*, 16 March 1986

The Divine Comedy (1996)

'This is the best complete rhymed Dante we are likely to have for a very long time, and one for which all readers of poetry will be profoundly grateful.' – David Wheatley, 'Rhyming His Way Between Heaven and Hell', *The Irish Times*, Dublin, 29 January 1997

Poems of François Villon (2001)

'Peter Dale has, while remaining faithful to the originals, produced wonderfully inventive, skilful, and above all, entertaining versions of Villon's masterpieces ... as well as the handful of other poems. In almost every line he has managed to find a modern English equivalent for the jaunty, often ribald and punning language of the original while sustaining a fine lilting measure that echoes the music of the French verse. This is a book to read and re-read.' – Vernon Scannell, 'Poète Maudit and Poems of Illness', *The Sunday Telegraph*, 29 July 2001

Poems of Jules Laforgue (2001)

'... [No] single volume in English ... can compete with Dale's virtuoso transposition of Laforgue, retaining so much of rhyme and rhythm, capturing so much of the French poet's subtlety of tone. Like the Villon, this deserves a place on any shelf of modern English verse translations.' – Glyn Pursglove, 'Poetry Comment', *Acumen*, 41, September 2001